PROFESSIONAL POWER AND THE NEED FOR HEALTH CARE

For Joy, Ffion and Cian

Professional Power and the Need for Health Care

IAN REES JONES
Faculty of Healthcare Sciences
St George's Hospital Medical School and Kingston University

Ashgate

Aldershot • Brookfield USA • Singapore • Sydney

Published by
Ashgate Publishing Ltd
Gower House
Croft Road
Aldershot
Hants GU11 3HR
England

Ashgate Publishing Company
Old Post Road
Brookfield
Vermont 05036
USA

British Library Cataloguing in Publication Data
Jones, Ian Rees
    Professional power and the need for health care. -
    (Developments in nursing and health care)
    1. Health care reform - Great Britain - Philosophy 2. Health
    care reform - Economic aspects - Great Britain 3. Health
    planning - Great Britain - History 4. Medical care - Great
    Britain - Needs assessment 5. Health attitudes - Great
    Britain
    I. Title
    362.1'0941

Library of Congress Catalog Card Number: 99-72601

ISBN 1 85972 626 7

Printed and bound by Athenaeum Press, Ltd.,
Gateshead, Tyne & Wear.

Contents

Figures and tables

Preface

When Margaret Thatcher wrote in the foreword to *Working for Patients* that the patients needs will always be paramount, the irony of that statement was felt by many inside and outside the National Health Service. Despite this, she was not the first nor the last to use a needs based rhetoric to support a particular ideology. This book is concerned with the language of need, the limits to our understanding of health needs and the consequences of those limitations. In it I attempt to present a critical account of the role of professional power in the UK health system. Theories of need, justice and rights are reviewed in relation to the structural changes the National Health Service experienced in the early 1990s under the Conservative governments NHS reforms. In this sense I examine recent events from the position of having engaged with and to a very small extent participated in some of those events. I am all too aware that this is a dangerous course of action. When asked to summarise the impact of the French Revolution, Zhou Enlai is said to have replied that it was 'too soon to tell' The claims made in this book should be read with at least that dictum in mind and the analysis I present should be seen as an attempt to provide a critique of health policy in the NHS using a *particular* framework. This framework incorporates Doyal and Gough's 'Theory of Need' with Habermas' notions of the demise of the public sphere. An independent review of renal services in London is used as an exemplar concentrating on the needs assessment work of the review group and the decision making debates this review group engaged in. By using a Habermasian perspective to investigate the ways in which the language of need was used in debates the distorting effects of professional power are investigated. Finally, the findings from this exemplar are used to inform a discussion of the relationship between understandings of health care needs, rationing and rationality and the implications this has for health policy in the UK. Although I adopt a critical approach, the work of this review group was a remarkable achievement given the constraints it experienced. This achievement was due to the knowledge and commitment of the review group members. I believe however that the high quality of their work adds strength to the critique I develop in this book and in particular should raise questions about the nature of decision-making in the NHS.

This book would never have seen the light of day had it not been for the generosity and support of a number of people. I am indebted to Sarah Curtis, Len Doyal, Sheila Hillier, Netar Mallick, Graham Moon, Edward Oliver and Ann Taket for their advice and support, and to the members of the renal review group for their co-operation. I am grateful to Paul Higgs for his advice and encouragement.

1 Introduction

The NHS was originally set up on the basis that it would provide universal health care to all, free at the point of need. Webster (1995, 1998) and Harrison et al (1990) have argued in different ways that from the very beginning the NHS was very much a hasty compromise. Klein (1983) on the other hand (among others) argued that the NHS was conceived and born from a political consensus. Despite their differences these commentators appear to be in agreement on at least one thing and that is early descriptions of the NHS as a needs based service were more a product of rhetoric than reality. As we shall see the 'rhetoric of need' has unfortunately sustained the idea of a NHS born of political consensus when its history has been, and continues to be, one of conflict (Higgs 1993). It is well known that since its inception the concept of a 'free' service has been redefined and the ability of the system to respond to needs has been continually questioned. The image of the NHS as a universal service is however strongly supported by the British public. This may be due in no small part to marked improvements in the health of the British public over the course of the twentieth century. Explanations for improvements in health have been the focus for considerable debate. McKeown (1979) has argued that most of the improvements in life expectancy and in health status from the 17th century onwards can be attributed, in the main, to improvements in socio-economic conditions and not to the developments made in modern health care. His thesis has been criticised for understating the impact of local politics and public health interventions (Szreter 1988) and for underplaying the role of health services (Mercer 1990), particularly in the period after the inception of the NHS. A question mark still remains over the impact of modern medicine in this post war period, whether this is raised by the critiques of radical doctors (Cochrane 1971) or by those starting from a Marxist tradition (Doyal 1979). Whatever the arguments surrounding improvements in population health status since 1948 it is clear that these improvements have not meant the disappearance of inequalities in health. Indeed, inequalities in health have persisted (Townsend and Davidson 1982) and during the decade of the eighties these inequalities have been seen to increase and have been attributed to the relationship between poverty and health (Whitehead 1987, Marmot 1989, Phillimore et al 1994, Bartley Blane and Davey Smith 1998, Acheson 1998).

It is against this background that we should view any changes to the structure of the NHS system itself as well as what motivated these changes. The history of structural and organisation change in the NHS has been sketched by Roberts (1992) as a progression through three periods; the administrative period, the planning period and the management period. In the 1980s, when the system moved into the management period, questions began to be asked about, not only the structure of health service delivery, but also about the supply and demand for health care and the way that health care could be financed in the future (Culyer, Donaldson and Gerard 1988). Such questions were prompted by Conservative views of the NHS as an inflexible and wasteful bureaucracy. They were to be disappointed by reviews that argued against a radical reform of the financing of the NHS and so the Thatcher government turned towards radical initiatives on the structure of the NHS. The capacity of quasi-markets[1] to introduce competitive disciplines to the public sector offered an attractive solution to the problem (Enthoven 1991), and led to the NHS reforms of 1991.

Structural reforms and their impact on needs

From 1st April 1991, District Health Authorities (DHAs) had to set up contracts for health services with providers (Hospitals, Community services, NHS Trusts and Directly Managed Units (DMUs), private and voluntary sector providers) on the basis of an assessment of the health care needs of their residents. General Practitioner fundholders were also allowed to contract for a limited set of health services, independently of DHAs. This arrangement was termed the 'purchaser provider split' where purchasers bought services on behalf of their residents or practice populations and providers sold their services in return for payments made from the purchasers' limited budgets. Negotiations for the buying and selling of services were undertaken through what was called the contracting process. In most cases departments of public health took on the role of 'needs assessors' for the purchasing authorities. Although *Working for Patients* [*wfp*] (DoH 1989a) did not consider public health needs assessment in detail, the relationship between public health and needs can be traced back to the Acheson report (Acheson 1988), which called for regular reviews of the population's health. The question of how needs assessment and purchasing

2

health care were to be linked was addressed by the Department of Health (*Secretary of State* 1989; EL 1990) concentrating initially on an epidemiological approach to needs assessment. This was given a critical dimension by the work of Stevens (1991) who related Need (defined as what people benefit from) to Demand (defined as what people ask for) and Supply (defined as what is provided). The Department built on this by developing a three pronged approach to needs assessment, based on epidemiological, comparative and corporate approaches to health needs, (DoH 1991) as a basis for contracts. This approach was not without its critics however and some argued that health care should not be purchased on the basis of total needs assessment but on economic evaluations of competing demands for resources (Donaldson and Mooney 1991). In this way, it was argued, 'rational' decisions could be made about where resources should be allocated. It was never clear therefore, what needs assessment in the reformed NHS should amount to, and there was and is still confusion concerning how resources can be allocated to services by means of contracts according to estimates of need.

The NHS reforms provided an opportunity to develop processes for need assessment in the health care arena, but the Department of Health gave no guidance as to the theoretical basis for this work. As a result, much of the early work was based on a 'synthetic' epidemiological approach, applying estimates of disease incidence and prevalence to local populations. Whilst such an approach was useful, its relevance to the experiences of individuals and groups receiving care was limited. In addition there seemed to be no apparent attempt to link this work to a theory of needs and more significantly to operationalise a theory of needs in health terms, so that results of the work could be channelled into effective purchasing. These deficiencies were highlighted by Frankel (1991) when he delineated the confusion surrounding the term 'health needs assessment'. This confusion stemmed from a number of different imperatives that influenced the relationship between 'needs' and the provision of health care. The public health imperative was concerned with total population needs and developing strategies based on prevention and health promotion. The economic imperative was concerned with marginal met needs and the most efficient ways of meeting needs, whilst the political imperative was one of reconciling a welfare system to the demands of free market ideology. In the midst of this an understanding of the relationship between the human subject and the system was in danger of being marginalised and the extent of this marginalisation seemed to be related to the lack of recognition given by health policy to the relationship between health and rights (Jones 1995). That is to say, policy was not grounded in any formal recognition of a relationship between needs and entitlements. On the contrary there seemed to be a deliberate muddling of the issue so that an already fragmented system was unable to take responsibility for the needs of those it was designed to serve.

The problem of need and scarcity

The 1980s saw many debates concerning the relationship between needs and welfare provision (Doyal and Gough 1984, Geras 1983, Wiggins and Dermen 1987, Soper 1981). The debate focused on absolute, normative and relative definitions of need, and discussed them in terms of their implications for political economy. Others used this debate to redefine the concept of need in economic terms (Culyer and Wagstaff 1991). Even those who argued for substantive needs, recognised that there are instances (particularly in areas like the provision of health care) where the concept of needs breaks down (Braybrook 1987, Thomson 1987) but that these instances can provide valuable insights into the dilemmas that surround the concept and the implications this has for health policy. The fair and just allocation of scarce health care resources according to need, requires a theory of need that calls on appropriate principles of justice and equity and can be operationalised within the system, but such an idealised approach falls on barren ground unless the problem of scarcity is addressed at the same time. How and whether suitable and appropriate principles of justice are embedded in the NHS is unclear. The NHS is funded from taxation and works in the main by means of allocating capped budgets by a central bureaucracy. Given budgets are limited it is axiomatic that rationing is necessary. Those who argued and still argue in favour of markets in the NHS, state that rationing has always gone on but the introduction of markets means that the criteria for rationing become more explicit and thus rationing itself will be fairer and more objective. If rationing is inevitable, it is not clear how the action of making it more explicit automatically leads to it becoming fair and objective. Doyal and Gough (1991) addressed this issue in their theory of need which has substantive and procedural elements. The theory is centred on the individual's capacity to participate in social life. They state that the two most basic needs are physical health and autonomy forming the preconditions for participation in moral life. Their argument focuses on a negative definition of health based on survival and avoidance of harm. Health care, in this theory, is a specific satisfier of the need for health and autonomy. This is the basis for the substantive part of the theory. In the procedural part they utilise Habermas' idea of the validity of human interests stemming only from agreement in free and open communication. For Doyal and Gough, agreement over needs and prioritisation between competing needs can only be legitimate if debates are grounded in this Habermasian approach.

4

The arguments presented in this book owe much to the theory developed by Doyal and Gough. The book does not aim to test Doyal and Gough's theory of human need but to use it and the Habermasian framework it draws on, to evaluate policy making processes at a particular point in time. In doing this the relevance of Doyal and Gough's theory for health policy in the UK should become clear. The next chapter will review arguments concerning 'objective', universal needs in the context of health care. If universal needs exist, can they form a basis for health policy and if so how can they be measured to inform this policy? I will address alternative notions of need as a basis for health policy, ranging from the new right, health economics and relativist notions of need. Definitions of need as a function of an individual's capacity to benefit will be reviewed together with the values that underpin such an approach. The 'objectivity' of economics will be questioned in light of this. In contrast I will make a distinction between the need for health and the need for health care and relate Doyal and Gough's paradigm of need to the health care system and consider a framework for assessing health care needs based on Doyal and Gough's concepts of health and autonomy. Following on from this, principles of justice will be considered in relation to health care from the viewpoint of the new right, health economics, Marxist, communitarian, feminist and liberal thinkers. I will draw on the relationship between needs and rights to argue with Doyal and Gough that in striving for a just system, their framework for assessing needs must, in turn, be based on procedures that rely on communicative ethics. I follow a path illuminated by Doyal and Gough's work and turn to the work of Habermas (1984) as a potential source of a theoretical basis for the communicative justice the health care system requires.

This review is not presented as an original *theoretical* contribution to the needs debate but as a background to inform my interpretation of the ways in which different understandings of need were employed in practical settings. Having set out the bases for the theoretical debate I outline Doyal and Gough's theoretical framework and consider its potential for evaluating needs assessment in the NHS. I reflect on the implications that a theory of need has for health policy, focusing in particular on the development of quasi-markets in the UK. I look at the history of policy explanations in the context of health care and relate four major theoretical perspectives; pluralist, public choice, elitist and Marxist, to the theory of human needs. I look at the theoretical background to the development of quasi-markets in health care and consider the implications of this development for the system. I focus on the importance of theories of power for any understanding of health policy and highlight the relevance of Habermas' communicative ethics to an analysis of decision making in the NHS. Habermas' condition for universality is consensus arising from an ideal speech situation and Doyal and Gough base the procedural part of their theory on this idea. Habermas' theory of communicative action presents a means for evaluating the ways in which needs are discussed in the public domain. It is the potential that Habermas' approach has for evaluating debates concerning needs in the health care system that I will explore.

I will introduce an exemplar based on a case study of a review of renal services in London. This was undertaken by an independent review group as part of the process of implementing the Tomlinson proposals for rationalising health care in the capital (Tomlinson 1992). My focus will be the process of policy making with respect to renal services and the extent to which discussions concerning health needs acted as a rational basis for decision making. The review was undertaken in the four months between March and June 1993 as one of the six speciality reviews established by the London Implementation Group (LIG) set up in the wake of the Tomlinson report. The renal review group reported in June 1993 and made recommendations on the future of renal services in the Thames Regions (Renal review group report 1993). Not all of the review group's recommendations were accepted or implemented. However, the London Strategic Review (Turnberg 1997) noted that for renal services:

> Five tertiary centres in London were planned with 5 specialist centres in the Thames Regions. This has been achieved in the North Thames Regions and in South East London. Consolidation of services at St George's Hospital and the St Helier Hospital has yet to be agreed. (Turnberg 1997, p. 22)

The ways in which the recommendations were received and acted upon is an important area for study but the focus of this book is on the quality of the debates undertaken during the period of the review. To develop my arguments on decision making and needs assessment therefore I will concentrate on the group's technical assessment of the need for renal services in the four Thames Regions, covering a population of some 14 million people. Having set out the evidence of need presented in the case study I will consider the quality of debates concerning health care need in relation to the 'democratic' and 'rational' nature of discussions. This will be done by means of an analysis of minutes of the group's meetings with renal units and transcripts of taped meetings of the review group where decisions about the future pattern of services were made. My stance will be a critical one but I should emphasise that the review group report was considered by many to be a remarkable achievement given the constraints the group were acting under. This achievement was due to the knowledge and commitment of the review group members. In a sense however, the high quality of their work adds strength to the critique I develop in this book and in particular should raise questions about the quality of less public decision-making in the NHS.

The research methods used in this work were based on an understanding of depth hermeneutics (Pile 1990). Using the three phases of social analysis, discourse analysis and interpretation I construct a narrative moving from the technical assessment of need made by the review group through to an analysis of debates concerning needs. I conclude by presenting a critique of health policy in the NHS based on Habermasian notions of the demise of the public sphere. I focus particularly on the systemisation of the life world by means of distorted communication that is characterised by the use of technocratic and arcane language by powerful interest groups. I argue that the ability of interest groups to override needs based arguments and even to use needs based arguments to promote particular interests, remained a dominant characteristic of the system. The drive towards competition and markets presented a challenge to interest groups but I argue that this contained a duality because of the capacity of market processes to reinforce the power base of certain interest groups. An important aspect of this is the way in which the medicalisation of need is both a means by which the 'systemworld' colonises the 'lifeworld' and a means by which challenges to the existing order can be made. These challenges were however held fast by the medical framework within which they were formed. I argue that quasi-markets appeared to play an important role in reinforcing this process. Finally, I draw conclusions about the practicalities of grounding health services in a theory of need and the implications of such an approach for evaluating the health system's role as a specific satisfier of health care needs.

Note

1   The term quasi-markets refers to the separation of supply and demand within an organisation. The terms internal markets and managed markets are also commonly used to describe such a system.

2 Health care needs, justice and rights to health care

> to render available to every individual all necessary medical service, general and specialist, and both domiciliary and institutional. (Beveridge Report, 1942 paragraph 427)

> The Patients needs will always be paramount. (Margaret Thatcher 1989, foreword to *Working for Patients*)

In this chapter my intention is to map the relationship between theoretical and practical understandings of health care needs on the one hand and the determination of policy on the other. I wish to explore the nature of our understandings and interpretation of health care needs and their capacity to both inform policy decisions and legitimate policy making. I structure the chapter by contrasting concepts of need and justice that have been developed by the New Right[1] and health economics[2] with a wider debate concerning the philosophical basis for a needs based health care system. I do this because health policy in the UK has been influenced by key ideas from these two separate, sometimes conflicting, but influential strands of thought. I use my critique of these approaches as a basis for considering the possibilities Doyal and Gough's theory of human need (Doyal and Gough 1991) holds for health care needs assessment. Doyal and Gough have constructed a theory of human needs based on the notion of basic needs being health and autonomy, an optimum[3] level of which is fundamental to allow participation in social lie. Soper (1993) is attracted to the theory at this general level but argues that as the theory becomes more exact and moves on to intermediate needs and the specific satisfiers for these needs then their 'universality' becomes more problematic. Sheaff (1996) on the other hand sees the 'fragility' of any claim to universal needs and attempts to develop a theory of needs based on human drives. My aim will be to show that whilst there are strong theoretical arguments for accepting the existence of

8

universal human needs at a general level, the project of maintaining such a universal position becomes more difficult as we begin to specify particular needs; health care being a prime example in this respect. If health care resources are to be allocated according to 'need' therefore, we require a procedural framework for discussing needs together with what constitutes a 'just' distribution of resources. After reviewing various approaches to justice, I emphasise the importance of Habermas' communicative ethics, not only for Doyal and Gough's theory but for understanding the problem of 'need' in the NHS.

Health care planning and the problem of human need

It is important to distinguish between the need for health and the need for health care. Health care is a satisfier that is one way in which we can meet our need for health. The need for health has been perceived by Acheson (1978) as relief from the negative states of distress, discomfort, disability handicap and the risk of mortality and morbidity. These concepts form the basis of but do not wholly determine the need for health services. This amounts to a biomedical approach to health care needs and as such it excludes positive concepts of health and health promotion. The approach is popular because it lends itself to quantitative measurements of health status, and the resulting health care needs fit conveniently with the biomedical focus on the incidence and prevalence of disease. Bradshaw (1972) on the other hand has constructed a paradigm of need in terms of normative, felt, expressed and comparative need. This forms a sociological approach to needs that sets up a useful matrix of the ways in which needs can be defined. However, as Bradshaw points out in a later piece (Bradshaw 1994), this was never intended as a way of constructing a hierarchy of needs. Indeed, Bradshaw argues that the concept of need is too imprecise and fraught with difficulties as to be a useful basis for health policy.

Arguments surrounding needs and health care have tended in the past to concentrate on the relationship between needs and service use and how the burden of needs interacts with the demand for, and access to, services (Titmuss 1968, Hart 1971, Last 1963). In this sense need is not an absolute concept, but is relative and dependent on socio-economic and cultural factors as well as supply side factors. It is here that arguments have developed around the effect of supply and demand on need (Eddy 1984, Friss et al 1989) and a questioning of the appropriateness of subjective value judgements of third party needs assessors as an alternative to consumer sovereignty (Culyer 1976). The nebulous nature of 'need' and its formulation as an antithesis to consumer preference theory has also formed the basis of the New Right's view of need, which sees attempts to determine needs as the first steps towards authoritarianism.

Need and the New Right

The New Right are not a homogenous group of thinkers and there are a number of streams of thought which can be described as New Right in origin. However, there are common elements to the approach of the New Right to the concept of needs and health care needs. Firstly, the New Right see the expression of individual preferences through the market mechanism not only as a more effective means of distributing resources, but also as having moral superiority over any attempt to plan on the basis of need. Secondly, the libertarian stream within the New Right equates personal health with individual responsibility as a means of promoting the ideal of 'self ownership'. This can be seen in Hayek's (1944) arguments concerning the link between markets and freedom, and Nozick's (1974) attacks on taxation, setting limits on its legitimacy as a means of supporting welfare provision.

Within health care, the New Right have approached needs with suspicion. Whilst arguments against objective, universal needs are not exclusively those of the New Right, their critique characteristically places an emphasis on the individual. Green (1986) argues that:

> medical 'need' cannot be objectively measured or predicted, and resources allocated to match. Any decision about whether or not to proceed with some recommended course of treatment entails judgements which touch upon intimate personal matters such as willingness to endure pain, face risks and, not least incur costs in the light of alternatives on which money might be spent. (p. 95)

The New Right therefore deny the existence of objective health care needs arguing instead that individual feelings about treatment decisions will vary considerably. There are tensions within the New Right however; Harris (1988) for one argues that:

> The trouble is that kindness corrupts, and in the end can even kill. Once policy departs from concentrating state help on the declining minority in quite specific forms of absolute need, the categories of prospective beneficiaries multiply and 'need' assumes an elastic dimension in the name of relative poverty (p. 18)

Some of the New Right therefore argue that some form of decent minimum requirement exists in terms of absolute basic needs. Thus their argument often seems to contradict those who argue against needs in any sense.

Perhaps the most damaging attack on the concept of 'health needs' and the ability of the NHS to meet 'needs' came from Enoch Powell (1966). Powell focused on the demand for health care and emphasised the role of price in the process of translating needs into demand for services. He argued that demand for health care was infinite where there were no price barriers to care, as in the NHS. Buchanan (1965) laid the ground for this attack by setting out two principles in support of a theory of infinite demand. The first was the elasticity principle which states that when price elasticity of demand is greater than zero, then individuals will demand more goods provided by public services than they would if those services were provided at a price in the market. The second principle is that of external economies whereby if externalities exist, these can be internalised in a publicly provided service but result in under-investment in a market system. He argued that these principles had a 'mutually reinforcing' effect and therefore would have expected that subsequent to the creation of the NHS there would have been a marked increase in public spending and provision relative to what would have been spent under a market system. He argued that this did not happen in the UK because the relationship between 'needs' and infinite demand was strictly controlled:

> The British experience strongly suggests that, rather than responding to 'needs' through increases in aggregate supply, governments have chosen to allow the quality of services to deteriorate rapidly, both in some appropriate physically measurable sense and in terms of congestion costs imposed on prospective customers. (p. 9)

The New Right therefore succeeded in the past in arguing against the concept of 'needs' whilst simultaneously chastising welfare state institutions (such as the NHS) for failing to respond to 'needs'. This reflects a fundamental problem with the New Right's approach in that by promoting the superiority of individual preferences and the moral force of the market they imply the existence of needs. Arguments that reject need are therefore contradictory in that they imply the existence of need. Arguments for basic needs on the other hand seem to be an attempt to reconcile the New Right's nebulous view of need with the need to specify some 'objective' basic minimum as an absolute standard. This again implies the existence of a universal objective notion of need, but fails because the 'decent minimum' is so clearly based on subjective notions of what a democratic free market system can tolerate. Perhaps in view of these difficulties, Gray (1992)

11

develops an argument for a social market economy with an enabling welfare state, based on a central premise of 'satiable basic needs'.[4] To develop his argument Gray draws on the work of Raz (1986) and the value given to autonomy as a basic need. Gray's arguments are particularly interesting when applied to health care:

> Raz illuminates a fundamental property of basic needs, as distinct from wants or preferences, when he notes that, most of them, in principle, are capable of complete satiation. The needs of the disabled, or of the illiterate, though sometimes perhaps expensive to meet, can be met completely, that is to say, to the point at which they can lead reasonably autonomous lives. (p. 66)

Gray recognises that with respect to medical care there are difficulties :

> Medical care generates peculiarly difficult problems...in that by no means all medical needs are fully satiable. Whereas those of the disabled are usually fully satiable, those connected with the process of ageing, or with illnesses that are terminal but which can (with an ever worsening quality of life) be indefinitely staved-off, sometimes are not. (pp. 66-7)

Gray points out that the policies put forward by the New Right, such as voucher schemes are guilty of the same indeterminancies that have been applied to 'needs'. Using school vouchers as an example he points out:

> what should be the size of a school voucher, and how (and by whom) is this to be determined? (p. 68)

This returns us to the dilemma of how to reject an objective notion of needs whilst at the same time presenting a case for satiable basic needs. Gray seems to find a solution to this problem by arguing that the characteristics of satiable basic needs are such that the goods necessary for their satiation can be defined by the agent in need:

> The deeper objection concerns the commensurability of basic needs. Among medical needs, can the preservation of life be ranked against the alleviation of pain? And how are medical needs to be weighed against educational or intellectual needs? It would seem that such judgements could be made, if at all, only by invoking a thick and comprehensive conception of the good life about which there is, among us, no consensus.

Distribution according to basic needs would then be arbitrary, in that it would impose on all a conception of the good life that was only one of several, possibly incommensurable conceptions harboured in our society. What can be said against this claim? An answer can be found I believe, in the fact that the content of a basic need is subject to partial self-definition by the agent. A person may have basic medical needs which require residence in a nursing home, but the detailed mixture of goods and services may again be determined by the person himself. (p. 68)

Gray seems to take this line of thinking to be sufficient to justify vouchers in that vouchers are in this sense a species of welfare benefit that is akin to a positive right. In a sense the idea of the voucher is introduced as a way of avoiding the 'paternalistic' characteristics of basic needs that the New Right object to. The New Rights approach to need is therefore twofold; either need is rejected completely, or some form of decent basic minimum is postulated, provided this is underpinned by concepts of individual choice and freedom.

Another flaw in the New Right approach can be found in their idealisation of the relationship between consumer sovereignty and human interests (Penz 1986). There are many diverse conceptions of human interests but the main thrust of consumer sovereignty sees what is produced, how it is produced and how it is distributed, as determined by consumer preferences expressed through individual choices in a free market. Even if we accept that consumer preferences revealed through the market are a plausible representation of the interests of individuals in production and distribution, this still leaves open the question of what these interests are. Seen in these terms consumer sovereignty has a normative centrality, it:

> is not a goal that competes with other primary goals of economic policy but rather a core value that underlies the most important economic policy goals in liberal or social democracies.(Penz 1986, p. 12)

However, in order that individuals are to reveal preferences a range of choices is required and this presents a problem in terms of how wide a range of choices is necessary. Penz argues that there is a trade-off between variety and quantity in that standardisation in production gives greater quantity of output for the same input but this is done at the expense of variety. Welfare economics tries to avoid the conflicts in this trade-off by focusing on efficiency. However, there are problems with the efficiency conception of consumer sovereignty because of an inability to distinguish between inefficient sovereignty and sovereignty constrained by other sovereign powers. Within health care where individual consumer sovereignty is at best compromised by a plethora of factors such as the agency relationship (Arrow 1963), lack of information and inability to discount risks, these arguments weaken considerably the New Right's approach to health care need.

The economics of need

Traditionally economists have been suspicious of attempts to define needs. Culyer (1976) pronounced that the word 'need' ought to be banished from discussion of public policy. Williams (1978) also argued that 'need' confused matters. More recently however economists have argued in terms of 'marginal met needs' resulting in the somewhat contradictory position where health economists have been the most vociferous in advocating health services be allocated on the basis of need. Indeed in talking about the NHS reforms Culyer, Maynard and Posnett (1990) argue:

> This reform has been influenced considerably by the work of economists who have long advocated that care should be allocated on the basis of need and that the efficiency of resource use be improved by the explicit measurement of costs and outcomes. (p. 1)

Economists have therefore developed arguments that accept 'needs' provided they are placed within an economic context. Culyer (1991) is open about this tactic :

> on the 'if you can't beat 'em join 'em ' principle (but only on *my* terms), it becomes necessary - stick though it may in the gullets of many economists to do so - to provide the word [need] with suitable content (p. 14)

The economic approach to needs in general and health care needs in particular is based on the concept of marginal met needs[5] (Steel 1981) manifested in arguments put forward in support of economic evaluation or 'marginal needs assessment' as it is sometimes called. Donaldson and Mooney (1991) argue that there are fundamental flaws in the concept of total or epidemiological needs assessment on the following grounds :

> -'need' per se is a red herring, *changes in 'need' met (or marginal met need)* being the relevant outcome factor on which to focus;
> - failure to account for the *responsiveness* of disease to health care interventions;
> -failure to account for *changes in costs and benefits* resulting from interventions. (p. 10)

The economic approach therefore uses the idea of the subjectivity of 'needs' to postulate an alternative paradigm of 'need'. Because of the 'subjectivity' of needs, the process of needs assessment is inevitably value laden, given that opinion on a patient's needs is usually made by a third party (usually a doctor). This argument about the subjectivity of needs and the superiority of individual preferences expressed through demand as measures of the appropriateness of health services underpins the economic approach and mirrors some of the arguments developed by the New Right. The argument is however, more complex than this. Economists see the 'objectivity' of need as patronising and dangerous but with respect to health care they concede that the agency relationship[6] (Arrow 1963), undermines the reliability of preferences. Economists therefore work towards making preferences more reliable and making needs assessment less patronising by opening it up to 'rational economic analysis'.

Culyer and Wagstaff (1991), consider the relationship between economic evaluation and need in detail. Their main concern is with the allocation of resources and the relationship between the two principles of 'distribution according to need' and equality of resources. They argue that the two principles are not linked and that any allocation of resources according to the principle of 'distribution according to need' does not automatically result in equality and may indeed result in greater inequality. What is significant to the present discussion is that to make their case Culyer and Wagstaff set up an economic definition of need which gives greater weight to the concept than previous economic approaches. Culyer and Wagstaff begin their analysis as sceptics of any attempt to construct a universal concept of need that embraces common meanings of the word. Instead they proffer a precise definition of need that relates specifically to health care:

> Instead of defining the need for medical care relative to some pre-specified end-state, we define it simply in terms of improving (or maintaining) health. A need for medical care is then said to exist so long as the marginal product of care is positive, i.e. so long as the individual's capacity to benefit from medical care is positive. We define an individual's level of need as the amount of medical care required to reduce the marginal product of care (or equivalently the individual's capacity to benefit) to zero. Clearly, "need" so defined is not synonymous with capacity to benefit...but rather is a function of capacity to benefit, depending too on the productivity of medical care at the margin. (p. 6)

The result of this is that they set themselves in opposition to Thomson (1987) who has argued that there is an 'element of practical necessity' in any normative use of 'need'. They argue that Thomson's approach is flawed because there are practical implications to his argument which he fails to address. Despite this it is important not to lose sight of Thomson's attempt to relate the denial of a need to a consequence of 'serious harm'. For Thomson, need is at the core of moral debate and should determine our moral judgements. The identification of a fundamental need forces us to pass from the *is* statement 'there is a need' to the *ought* statement 'the need ought to be met'.

Seeing needs in instrumental terms requires that the 'end states' or 'goals', towards which needs are instrumental, be examined. Culyer and Wagstaff again see problems here citing the various end states that have been put forward such as freedom and autonomy (Wiggins and Dermen 1987), life and health (Braybrook 1987). They also argue that the attempt by Wiggins and Dermen to develop a categorical concept of need, fails because it appeals to the ethical force of the ends. In terms of health being a goal they argue that where health is seen as a binary variable i.e. sick or healthy then this gives rise to a binary interpretation of need. The binary interpretation of need, it is argued, puts needs in conflict with the construction of health and health care as continuous variables. If health is a continuous variable then the end point or goal towards which needs are instrumental, becomes elastic and nebulous. These arguments lead them to conclude that a necessary condition for a need is that if what is needed is provided it should result in a person moving towards the goal or end state required. From this they conclude that with respect to health care then if the satisfying of a 'need' has a very small or negative impact on the end state, namely health, then the 'need' cannot be needed. For a need to exist, therefore, some positive productivity in response to the need is a necessary prerequisite. This is not all of the picture however, for they argue that there may be more than one way of achieving this positive productivity, and therefore cost-effectiveness has a role to play in this process. Allied to these points, they argue that to be sick is not a necessary precondition of being in need. This statement allows the possibility for being in need of preventive services, as well as the situation where an individual is so sick that no amount of health care will improve their condition.

The problem with the approach is that ultimately need is equated with the productivity of the good identified for satisfying that need. A person is only in need of health care if health care can produce positive benefit; need is a function of supply. What are the implications of this for improving health care and identifying needs?   There is a danger that needs may go unrecognised whilst health care does not presently exist to produce benefits in response to those needs. More importantly, the raw materials that health

16

care is interacting with to produce a benefit are not homogenous units that react in predictable ways. Seedhouse (1994) sees the benefit definition of health care need as bizarre in that the necessary condition of a person having a health care need is the existence of beneficial health care. If needs are defined by the services available to meet them, then increases in beneficial services lead to increases in need, thus making it impossible for needs to be reduced by meeting them with more services. It would also be possible to argue that in the past, when there was less health care and less beneficial services, then there were less needs. Similarly, where national and geographic boundaries place limits on access to health care, then in countries where the levels of health services are lower than others, under the benefit definition, it could be construed that there are relatively less needs. The limits placed on needs when they are defined in relation to productive processes within the parameters of time and space, should not be overlooked.

The economic definition of need is popular however because it enables conventional marginal product theory to adjudicate among competing claims for health care. When prioritising between goods the yardstick by which they should be judged should be the relative social value attached to the ultimate outcomes relative to other components of social welfare, thus allowing the value to society over and above the value to an individual to be included in the priority making process. The popularity of the definition of need introduced above is dependent on how 'benefit' itself is defined. There seems to be an implication that benefit, unlike need, is real and quantifiable or at least is more easily quantifiable. Are we in danger of substituting one difficult word (need) with another (benefit) to which we are ascribing a false sense of exactitude?

Needs as benefits

Economists view health benefits in terms of survival and quality of life:

> The most obvious effect of many health treatments is that the
> natural history of disease is changed for the better. That is life
> may be extended, or the quality of life may be improved.
> (Drummond 1980, p. 12)

The key concept is that such improvements can be examined at the margin thus allowing comparisons of incremental changes in benefits. Economists don't just see the consequences of these benefits in individual terms. They also argue that we all derive benefit from the health gain of others and that this should be accounted for as part of total social gain. Kilner (1990) examines four aspects of benefit; medical benefit, likelihood of benefit,

17

length of benefit and quality of benefit and shows that there are considerable problems with this approach. The attraction of medical benefit as a criterion for the allocation of scarce resources is clear. The pragmatic argument is that any medical intervention that does not work (i.e. has no benefits) is a waste of resources. This is different, however, to saying that resources should be allocated on the basis of the comparative medical benefits of different interventions. Such calculations are often made not on certain knowledge about benefit but on assessments of likelihoods, risks and subjective value judgements about quality. The subjectivity involved should remind us of economists complaints about the nebulous nature of 'needs'. The fundamental difficulty with the use of benefit as a criterion, therefore, is that it fails to supply a universally acceptable definition of what benefit means and how it can be measured. In this sense it suffers from the same criticism that economists have levelled at previous definitions of need in that, at best, benefit is dynamic and open ended.

The objectivity of economics

Health economists have been successful in promoting the benefit approach because the discipline has argued persuasively that decision making in health care should not be made on the basis of implicit value judgements of professional groups. Health Economics, it is argued, can make decision making explicit and thus paves the way for a fairer system of resource allocation. But economics is not value free. There are various schools of thought that represent differences of opinion on key economic issues from the role of the market in determining the distribution of resources to the impact of consumer preferences on the demand for primary goods. Within health economics too there are differences of opinion about the analysis of health care as an 'economic good', and about the effect of price and supply on the demand for health care. Arguments abound on a host of key areas such as assessing the value of life, the elasticity of demand and the impact of vertical and horizontal inequity.

Can the claim that economics offers an objective and rational approach to health care decision making stand up to scrutiny? Penz (1986) argues economic approaches to welfare are not objective because of 'evaluation circularity'. Evaluation circularity, as described by Penz, refers to the interactive loop between the institution and processes of production and the consumer preferences that form the basis for evaluating these institutions and processes. This is the process where instruments of economic measurement have an effect on that which is being measured and the thing being measured changes the economic instruments. As a result claims of economic objectivity and rationality are compromised.

What is being evaluated determines, in part, the criteria by which it is being evaluated. (Penz 1986, p. 87)

This is the fundamental weakness of any attempt to promote individual utility values as a means of identifying human interests. In the field of health care this weakness becomes a fatal flaw because of the nature of health and the extent of uncertainty. Avorn (1984), writing from the viewpoint of one concerned with discrimination and the elderly, argues that many of the methods employed by health economists:

embody a set of hidden value assumptions that virtually guarantee an anti-geriatric bias to this purportedly objective data. (Avorn 1984, p. 1295)

The problem is the base on which health economics works, namely utilitarianism which imports implicit valuations of productive worth. Assumptions are made about the validity of individual preferences and these assumptions are presented as an objective and rational basis for formulating policy decisions. Within these assumptions are a set of implicit value judgements, and in the rush to argue that economic methods make decision making more rational these implicit value judgements are often overlooked. Redefining need as a function of capacity to benefit does not relieve economics from the above criticisms. Instead it imprisons us in what Seedhouse calls a 'looking glass' logic (Seedhouse 1994 p. 29). It is these criticisms that should remind us that measurement of clinical benefits, whilst offering a useful guide for physician decision making at the level of the individual, imports a host of ethical and technical problems when operated at group level or at the level of society.

Health care as an intermediate need

Daniels (1985) attempts to characterise the relevant categories of needs in a way that *explains* two central properties that basic needs have:

1. That they are objectively ascribable i.e. they can be ascribed to a person even if she doesn't know they exist and even if they are contrary to her preferences.
2. They are objectively important; importance is given to the claims based on them in a variety of moral contexts, independently of the importance given to them by individuals.

The task for Daniels therefore is to define the things we need which have the above two properties. Daniels associates needs with normal species functioning. Need is related to harm and its effect on the normal species functioning so that:

> impairments of normal species functioning reduce the range of
> opportunity open to the individual in which he may construct
> his 'plan of life' or 'conceptions of the good'. (p. 27)

The implication of this argument for disease and health is considerable. Daniels starts with a narrow definition of health as the absence of disease. Disease is formulated as deviations from *natural* functional organisation of a *typical* member of species. This is a biomedical model of health and there are clear, well recognised problems with such an approach in that it tends to see diseases as deviations from social norms. There are problems with the definition of what is normal. Can we distinguish disease from genetic variations? What environments are 'natural'? An environment full of white racists, for example, could characterise being black as a disease. In order to avoid these criticisms, Daniels modifies the biomedical model to allow for some relativism by saying the line between disease and absence of disease is generally uncontroversial, and can be ascertained by means of publicly acceptable methods. The problem here is that this may be easier to achieve for some diseases than others. Getting agreement on a definition of mental illness is more problematic than this account suggests. A complete theory would have to establish what counts as health and what counts as disease as well as being able to prioritise between health care needs and other social and individual needs.

Liss (1993) sees need in terms of a gap between an actual state and a goal. If X is needed to enable a person to move from an actual state to a goal, then there is a need for X. This of course is dependent on further clarification of the nature of the goal in question. Doyal and Gough follow a path that is similar to Daniels in their theory of human need. In their interpretation of the statement 'A needs X in order to Y', the end state Y is not 'health' with all its associated definitional problems but the avoidance of serious harm which they equate with *minimally disabled social participation.* 'A needs X in order to Y' therefore becomes 'A needs *basic need satisfaction* in order to avoid *disabled social participation*'. Now the basic needs Doyal and Gough have in mind are health and autonomy and these give rise to a set of intermediate needs among which the provision of 'appropriate' health care is included. The link with Liss' account is the goal of participation in society, remembering that health care may or may not be the most appropriate means of achieving this goal. In terms of health care, therefore, the statement becomes, 'A needs appropriate health care in order to avoid disabled social participation'.

'Appropriate' health care, preventative, curative and palliative, is an intermediate need operationalised in terms of its effectiveness in optimising social participation, and minimising disabled social participation, relative to other intermediate needs. Health promotion is an important component of appropriate health care in that it aims to enhance levels of critical autonomy, that is; the ability of individuals to make healthy choices as well as criticise and challenge the range of choices available to them. Survival however, is the primary objective of health care for how can we participate if we are dead. This does not however exclude the possibility that a person may need to die, provided they are right in their belief that their capacity to flourish through social participation has ended (Doyal 1993).

Minimising disabled social participation is based on an interpretation of disability as standing between the medical construct of disease and the social construct of handicap in the sequence;

Disease ➡ Impairment ➡ Disability ➡ Handicap

In order to assess the need for health care, therefore, we need measures of disability and agreement over definitions of disability. Doyal and Gough refer to the OPCS work on the prevalence of disability in Adults (OPCS 1988) which used a ten point disability scale to support their approach. OPCS sought agreement on the definition of disability from a judgement panel of professionals, researchers, people with disabilities, carers and voluntary workers. The panel was asked to arbitrate on the severity of various conditions. Although imperfect, this was an attempt to develop agreement on the definition and measurement of disability in a publicly acceptable and accountable manner. For Doyal and Gough therefore, agreement on needs as defined in relation to disability requires a framework for open discussion of disability. The provision of health care as an intermediate need should be determined by reference to its capacity to minimise effectively, death and disability in that order. Doyal and Gough operationalise their theory using physical health, ill-health, autonomy and opportunities for economic activity as the components of basic needs that are measurable. A framework for these components is given in table 2.1.

This constitutes an attempt to define and measure physical health in negative terms as minimisation of death, disability and disease and to define and measure autonomy in negative terms as minimisation of mental disorder, cognitive deprivation and restricted opportunities. They consider the combination of these two negative definitions to approach a positive concept of well being. In later chapters I will use the components of basic needs framework to evaluate the work of the renal review group.

Doyal and Gough's conceptual framework has been applied in an audit of local needs in Leeds (Percy-Smith and Sanderson 1992). This audit demonstrated the relevance of Doyal and Gough's work to community based

Table 2.1
The components of basic needs

PHYSICAL HEALTH :
Survival chances
Mortality rates
Risk of death
Physical ill-health
Prevalence and severity of disability
Morbidity rates by disease categories
Pain
AUTONOMY
Mental disorder
Prevalence and severity of mental illness
Cognitive deprivation, literacy, attainment of basic skills, absence of skills
Opportunities for economic activity
Extent of employment
Free time
Extent of engagement in social interaction

Source: Doyal and Gough 1991; adapted from table 9.2, p. 190

understandings of need combining a 'bottom up' (using the views of local residents) and 'top down' (using expert and professional knowledge) approach to needs assessment. With respect to health care Doyal has emphasised the importance of the framework for evaluating the quality of services (Doyal 1992). When they consider the measurement of the intermediate need for health care, Doyal and Gough can only offer indicators of need that chart people's access to appropriate health care. These include direct indicators of health care provision (e.g. doctors/ beds per capita) and direct indicators of access to services (e.g. proportion of the population without access to community health services). This does not provide a sufficient basis for evaluating a health care system's capacity to address health care needs. In order to do this we must look at whether the components of basic needs are addressed and how they are defined and measured by the system. The problem of course, lies in the detail; in the extent to which we can define disability and come to agreement over the capacity of various health care interventions to be effective. The word 'appropriate' is important here in light of research showing variations in physician practice amidst different professional understandings of 'appropriate' health care interventions (Evans 1990). In addition, the normative definition of disabilities is not supported by some disabled groups; there are problems in defining the body in relation to social norms (Seymour 1989) and the cultural production of disability can understate the social determinants of handicap (Oliver 1990). Even survival presents difficulties for reaching agreement as the cases of persistent vegetative state have highlighted (Lancet 1993, editorial).

Operationalising health care in relation to minimally disabled social participation demands an openness in decision making. If we are to come to agreement over survival and disability, and which health care treatments are appropriate in meeting our goals, then a framework has to be found for discussing these issues in an open and fair manner. It is therefore important to examine principles of justice in relation to health care needs, and explore how we can build a framework for discussing the equitable distribution of health care resources.

Health care planning and the problem of equity

The publication of the Black report in 1980 re-focused health research on poverty and concentrated sociological and policy debates on inequalities in health. In the UK there is now a large body of work testifying to the growing health divide and addressing the question of how differences in health status between social classes should be tackled (Townsend 1993, Whitehead 1987). However, the question of *equity* in health care remains problematic. On a theoretical level, the principle of equity has received considerable attention from the New Right and from health economists. Economists have been particularly successful in highlighting the problems of the trade-off involved between goals of equity and efficiency (Le Grand 1990), and between distribution according to need and equality (Culyer and Wagstaff 1991). In this section I will address, in turn, the arguments put forward by the New Right and by health economists regarding equity, presenting a critique of their approaches based on the view that inequity follows directly from these theoretical positions. I will then consider a minimal criterion for justice based on Habermas' communicative ethics, showing how this links in with Doyal and Gough's work as a necessary procedural element to their theory of need. The policy implications of this, in terms of rights to health care, will be emphasised. To begin with however, it would be useful to reflect on what is meant by justice.

23

In *The Lottery in Babylon* Jorge Luis Borges describes a society where all social benefits and costs are distributed according to a periodic lottery.[7] This seems a bizarre social system, but there are clear parallels with contemporary arguments about rationing health care and welfare programmes where scarcity is a constraint. Many of the arguments surrounding rationing have been based on the view that present policies are unjust precisely because they amount to a lottery and there seems to be no basis in justice for such a system. Others have argued that what is required is some form of systematic lottery as a way of choosing between moral equals. Patients waiting for kidney transplants are in a queue for a scarce resource. The allocation of such scarce resources could be made on many differing bases (the highest bidder, individual preferences, merit, race, gender etc.). If we are to decide on which method is best then we need to refer to some standard of justice in order to make such a judgement. Merely stating that we need such a standard, however, does not free us from the relativist critique; there is no Archimedean position of absolute moral objectivity. But it does make it necessary for us to look around for the best basis for justifying our moral values and principles.

Marx criticised justice on the basis that standards of justice are internal to the economic and cultural characteristics of each society. Similarly he argued that rights embody the model of man as egoistic individual. The critique of justice as being embedded in existing productive relationships and determined by the ideology of the dominant class still has force (Wood 1981), but the ambiguities of Marx's approach to justice leaves questions over whether his critique focuses on a judicial paradigm of justice, thus leaving room for an appeal to an objective ideal of justice. It has been possible for justice to be dismissed by Marxists, particularly when it is argued that under communism, moderate scarcity (Hume's condition for justice), ceases to exist. This argument can be criticised on two counts. Firstly, conditions of scarcity exist as of now and, if we accept that time is a resource, then scarcity of opportunities for action will always exist (Buchanan 1982). Secondly, the approach does not tally with Marx's own critiques of capitalism, for if we are to judge whether a socialist society is better than a capitalist society, we need some standard of justice in order to make such an evaluation. Indeed, it has been argued that if Marx did not recognise the moral force of justice how was he then able to criticise capitalism (Peffer 1990).

Communitarians also have an ambivalence towards justice arguing that 'traditional universal' accounts of justice are inadequate, indeed can be harmful, and that a truly good community has no need for justice (Sandel 1984). A society is considered just by communitarians if it acts in line with the shared understandings of its members (Walzer 1990). Sandel (1982) sees family love and solidarity as institutions embodied in the community that make justice irrelevant. Indeed, the liberal preoccupation with justice is seen as harmful to those institutions. Walzer (1990) argues that the concept of 'objective justice' having a perspective from outside society is misguided and the requirements of justice is identified by the way each community understands the value of social goods. Justice is therefore specific to each community. Such arguments have been opposed by Cohen (1986) who argues that the values embodied in the free social institutions of communities, although idealised by Walzer, are often those of the powerful. In addition, if the institutions of communities are capable of reinforcing harmful practices and traditions, then communitarianism becomes essentially conservative. The communitarian framework could result in practices such as genital mutilation, for example, being justified under circumstances where the power structures and prevailing ideologies within a community presented genital mutilation as an acceptable and widely supported tradition. And supporting movements to eradicate such practices is not necessarily a form of euro-centrism or cultural imperialism.

Feminist critiques of justice see it as a male notion, inadequate to meet women's needs (Gilligan 1987). For women, morality is equated with responsibility and the protection of relationships in contrast to male notions of rights and abstract rules. Gilligan argues that to address this problem what is required is an ethics of care. Some have argued that the notion of care developed by Gilligan is already contained within justice particularly Rawls' theory of justice (Okin 1989), but liberal theories of justice have been criticised by some feminists for being subject to a historical commitment to a public/private distinction where the private sphere of the family has not been subject to principles of justice (Kearns 1983). Kymliska (1990) rejects this critique on the grounds that it conflates public/private, state/society and public/domestic, arguing that the problem of incorporating the role of the family is common to all theories of justice.

Despite the disagreements about justice outlined above, it would appear that they share a fundamental premise namely that the interests of the members of community matter and matter equally (Dworkin 1983). This premise is referred to by Dworkin as the 'egalitarian plateau'. Similarly Sen (1992) sees a basic common premise to disagreements about equality. With respect to health care the problem of what is considered a 'just' distribution of scarce resources is subject to this same 'egalitarian plateau'.

The New Right and justice

The New Right draw on entitlement theory to argue that justice is embedded in free markets. The championing of free markets results in arguments for health care to be distributed by means of the price mechanism on the basis that this results in a just allocation of health care resources. This argument is buttressed by entitlement theory (Nozick 1974) which states that individuals are entitled to what they have acquired provided it is acquired justly. This includes the inheritance of resources acquired justly by those who give them to us. In this sense distribution is determined largely by luck. Nozick proposes a night-watchman state, minimalist in character with its functions limited to protecting the rights and entitlements of its citizens. He rejects all material principles of justice in favour of the principle of self ownership. This states that each individual has full rights to self ownership and can acquire exclusive property rights to any part of the unowned world provided this does not make anyone else worse off. In his mind, the proper framework for the application of these principles is the free market. The theory is based on a weak interpretation of the Lockean proviso that acquisition of property is just, provided it does not make anyone worse off, but self-ownership is compromised when the rights of property owners are determined at the expense of restricting the freedoms of the propertyless. With respect to health care it is unclear whether the theory can operate in terms of our entitlement to levels of health or levels of health care. Persons are born with different levels of health, some are able bodied and become disabled, others are disabled from birth. They have acquired their health status through no fault of their own merely through the lottery of life. Entitlement theory at its crudest would seem to accept this state of affairs as just and would therefore oppose any attempt by a health care system to rectify the situation. Entitlement theorists would be entitled to object to this interpretation, and Nozick does argue that in cases of 'catastrophic moral horrors' entitlement rights could be modified, but this implies modification in extreme cases so the point with respect to health status still highlights a considerable weakness in entitlement theory. Individuals can choose some lifestyles that are less risky than others but the extent to which individual choices result in different health status is unclear and the impact of exogenous factors on individual health cannot be ignored. In light of this, the reductionist approach of entitlement theory seems inappropriate to any analysis of health care.

Nozick however is emphatic in his view that the right to health care is dependent on it being acquired through the market or voluntary charity. Attempts by the state to redistribute health care to the poor are therefore unjust. Nozick dismisses attempts to introduce the value of caring, compassion, externalities or uncertainties into the equation. It is with respect to the last two factors that the theory is most seriously flawed. It is doubtful whether a perfect market for health care which could act as a mechanism for an entitlement theory of health care, exists either in theory or reality. This can be seen with respect to persons who are in, or about to go into, end stage renal failure. Kidney patients could reasonably come under Nozick's definition of catastrophic moral horrors. However, kidney patients are continually faced with factors such as lifestyle choices, externalities and uncertainties which have an effect on their health status and their need for health care. Some of these factors will be wholly or partly within their control whilst others will be completely beyond their capacity to influence. The relationship between choice and control over factors that affect the health status of such patients is complex. Entitlement theory does not pursue an understanding of these complexities, instead it relies on the market as the most just method of allocating resources. In doing so it cannot avoid 'victim blaming' in the cases of persons who do not fit into its model of 'self ownership'.

The New Right have built on the foundations provided by Nozick and others to produce arguments that oppose attempts by the state to redistribute resources in a fairer manner. With respect to health care these arguments are employed to argue that the organisation of health care according to market principles is the best way of ensuring its fair distribution. This is based on the New Right equating the free market with liberty and is dependent on the notion that liberty is equated with the number of choices available to individuals (Gray 1988). However, it is unclear whether, and how, liberty could be measured by reference to the number of choices available. What is the value in choosing between a vast array of different dialysis machines for example? It seems unlikely that such a variety of choices extend our liberties in any way.

There are of course all kinds of problems associated with the extent to which health care is a good that can operate in a free market at a price, including consumer ignorance, the agency relationship and the value of social goods such as medical education. Light (1992) gives a detailed synopsis of how competitive markets are distorted in the field of health care. It is because of this that the approach of the New Right to justice in health care is flawed; entitlement theory cannot take account of the complex relationship between individual health status, access to health care and externalities.

Health economics and justice

The two main strands of economic approaches to equity in health care have been the health maximisation account and the equity as choice approach. A more recent strand based on Sen's (1992) capabilities approach has much in common with the arguments presented in this book. Each of these arguments will be considered in turn but first it is necessary to grasp the problem that equity presents for economics.

The economists concern for consumer sovereignty can sometimes result in a somewhat cavalier attitude to moral questions. Maynard for example has argued that:

> equity like beauty, is in the mind of the beholder. (Quoted in Pereira, 1990a p. 4)

Mooney and McGuire (1987) have also highlighted the numerous, sometimes conflicting, definitions of equity that can be used in relation to the distribution of health care resources. When looking at economic definitions of equity it is therefore important to understand the extent to which different strands of health economics relate to concepts such as consumer sovereignty and utilitarianism. Sen (1987) highlights the contradictions between utilitarianism and justice, emphasising that utilitarianism's concern with welfare is balanced by a lack of concern for the distribution of the sum of utilities. Economists view this criticism with varying degrees of concern; the extent to which the decreasing marginal utility of money is recognised being a crucial determinant of how economists see maximising utility conflicting with equality (Smith 1994). Nevertheless, Sen has succeeded in demonstrating that the consequentialism of utilitarian theory presents considerable problems with respect to equity.

The goal of health maximisation has been a means of avoiding these problems. It is argued that equity exists in a health care system where distributions serve to maximise health in society. The argument is so closely linked to basic utilitarianism however, that its inherent inequity is a clear problematic. There have been two main attempts to employ the health maximisation account, the first tries to take account of externalities whilst the second is the quality adjusted life year (QALY) approach. Culyer (1980) presented an argument for welfare maximisation by arguing that in measuring social welfare it is necessary not only to aggregate individual personal utilities but also necessary to take account of the utility individuals gained from knowing that the welfare of others is protected. This Culyer called the 'caring externality' which seems to appeal to notions of compassion (measured in terms of utility) as opposed to justice. Culyer attempted to move away from 'crass utilitarianism' by defining utility in a broad sense. The 'caring externality' therefore appears to be an attempt to 'buy off' the basic critique of utilitarianism by presenting us with a more sophisticated version of it.

The objective of health maximisation has also been presented in terms of QALYs.[8] This has been seen as a rejection of traditional Paretian welfare economics and a radical break from measuring utility. The QALY approach moves away from individual valuations of health and regards a QALY as having an equal value for everyone (Wagstaff 1991). This has led to the argument that whilst utilitarianism may not be concerned with the distribution of utilities merely the sum of utilities, QALYs are concerned with the distribution of QALYs. The problem with this is that QALYs of themselves are discriminatory[9] (Harris 1985). One argument has been to attach weights to QALYs to take account of these distributional problems. But this seems to go against the original argument in favour of the QALY which presented them as having the property of being equally valued by all, thus avoiding the criticisms of utility theory (Culyer and Wagstaff 1993).

If we turn to the definition of equity as equality of health it would seem that under this definition any reduction in inequality is a good thing. Wagstaff (1991) argues that the pursuit of the goal of equality of health does provide a basis for equitable allocation of resources but the principle conflicts with efficiency, and with health maximisation goals. How can these conflicts be reconciled? One approach suggested is to employ a social welfare function constructed to take account of society's objections to inequality allowing a trade-off between inequality and efficiency. It is clear that problems with defining equity will lead to problems in its pursuit in practice. If individuals value equity differently then different weights can be given to it as an objective of the health care system. In this sense equity is viewed only in terms of trading it off with other objectives, particularly efficiency. It is argued that equity and efficiency tend not to conflict in cases of horizontal equity and that the 'trade-off' becomes more acute in cases of vertical equity.[10] With respect to vertical equity there is a fundamental problem of prioritising on the basis of which patients are worse off (De Jong and Rutten 1983). This idea of a trade-off is an important part of the utilitarian debate. Implicit in the argument is the tendency to view equity as having a utility that allows it to be measured against the utility gained from efficiency.

Le Grand (1987) proposes a concept of equity in terms of equal constraints. Under this approach inequalities in levels of health are acceptable provided they are the result of choices made under the same constraints. Where variations in health status are the results of the 'lottery of life' or factors beyond individual control then we face an inequitable position, but where these variations are the result of life choices that are within the power of individuals to control then the variation is equitable. According to Le Grand, where rational individuals are facing equal choice sets then the outcome of their choices is equitable whatever the outcome in distributional terms. This has parallels with Nozick's entitlement theory. The argument is attractive because it recognises that individuals do face varying constraints and therefore some (e.g. people with low income) can have more limited choice sets. At an empirical level therefore the approach has great potential in measuring the different choice frontiers that individuals face and the factors that determine the limits to their choice sets. As has been stated previously, however, health care is an area where uncertainty and limits to consumer knowledge are magnified. The rational individual with perfect knowledge making autonomous choices on the basis of her preferences represents an economist's ideal rather than reality. Neither is it clear that an individual's choices result in direct trade-offs between healthy and unhealthy options. The application of the approach to health policy may result in the introduction of value judgements about the different constraints that are problematic in themselves. Le Grand however argues that his approach should not affect how people are treated by the health care system but could have a bearing on whether they ought to contribute towards financing their care e.g. smokers being given an extra tax. An alternative to this is the 'envy-free' approach to the distribution of resources which attempts to define an equitable distribution as a situation where relative individual positions are judged by the extent to which individuals would prefer to be in the position of others. In a two person economy for example an equitable distribution exists where one individual's utility for their own bundle of goods equals the utility value they place on the others bundle of goods and vice-versa. The appeal of this approach to the economists lies in its emphasis on individual preferences rather than by appeal to a moral theory. Again the approach is flawed because of its methodological individualism. Relative utility values cannot be relied upon to distinguish between demand for services by a person requiring hip replacement as opposed to a sports person's demand for sports equipment if both end up giving equal value to each others potential utility.

Economics fails to give an adequate basis for evaluating the fairness of a distribution. This stems from the ambivalence accorded to concepts such as 'need' and 'health'. If moral philosophers are correct in their assertion that basic health is a necessity for the goal of flourishing or a good life then need, capacity to benefit and income are not as important as equality of health. This leads Culyer and Wagstaff into a circular argument:

> if it is the ethical status of health as necessary for the leading of a 'flourishing' life that conveys any moral superiority to 'need' over mere 'demand', then it is also the same ethical force that makes need an insufficient distributional principle: the resultant distribution of health may not correspond to that required (whether equal or unequal) to ensure that each has a fair chance of leading a life that is as 'flourishing' as resources permit. (Culyer and Wagstaff 1992, p. 16-17)

This argument relies on the ambiguity of the word 'health' for its support. It skirts around the relationship between health as a basic need and justice. Kennedy (1983) reminds us that equity is a fundamental moral principle which is of critical importance with respect to health care. The problem with

30

economic approaches is that they either exclude justice completely or fail to take it seriously enough.

The basic capabilities approach

An approach that has taken many of the above criticisms on board is the basic capabilities approach, based on the work of Sen (1985, 1992) and applied to health care by Pereira (1990b). Sen argues that it is the capabilities of individuals to transform commodities into human functionings that is important. In this sense his argument owes much to Rawls (1972) whilst criticising what Sen calls Rawls' goods fetishism. By this he means that Rawls' theory places too much emphasis on goods in themselves rather than on what people can do with them.

In placing the emphasis on 'functionings' (how people use the characteristics of goods to produce human activities) Sen highlights the problems he sees in the link between functionings and utility. Individuals with low levels of functioning may have higher utilities than those with high levels of functioning. Clearly an analysis based on functionings is less open to the distortions of a utility based analysis. In addition there is a clear link between Sen's functionings and Doyal and Gough's needs that enable participation. In relation to equity Sen argues that it is capacity to function that is important and the equity principle can be summarised by 'equality of basic capabilities'. Within these basic capabilities Sen includes the ability to meet needs for food, clothing, shelter and good health. With respect to health care an individual's capacity to function will be dependent on access to basic goods and her personal capacity to interact with those goods to optimise her functionings. Equity can then be said to exist when individual capacities to use the characteristics of goods to achieve a desired function are equal. The approach is open to similar criticisms that have been laid at the door of Le Grand's equity as choice theory namely that some choices may be due to individual tastes whilst others are exogenous and due to societal/biological constraints. The problem is in the extent to which it is possible to differentiate between the two types of choices. Nevertheless, the basic capabilities approach represents a major step in the economic sense towards taking the concepts of justice and equity seriously. Clearly for a theory to provide the basis for an equitable health care policy it must recognise the relationship between functioning, impairment and human rights. It is useful therefore to consider different philosophical approaches to equity.

Philosophical approaches to equity

Liberal theories of justice have been re-examined in recent years from a variety of philosophical positions. A major focus for this has been Rawls theory of justice (Rawls 1972).[11] Justice, for Rawls depends on how well it does by its least advantaged participants. Rawls' theory is a theory of rights and justice which implies a social policy whose goal is to maximise the position of the least well-off. Rational individuals acting under a 'veil of ignorance' about their relative positions in society would choose a policy that would maximise the position of the worst off. The theory is postulated in terms of a set of 'primary social goods', health care not being one of them. It is important to note that Rawls excluded health care because he wished to avoid trade-offs with other primary goods such as income.

Rawls' theory has been criticised by Dworkin (1981) on the grounds that the difference principle is applied to groups not individuals. He proposes an alternative based on equality of resources whereby an equal share of resources be allocated to each individual on the basis of the opportunity cost of such an allocation to others. He argues that the liberal concept of equality is fundamental, and that rights to particular liberties are dependent and derivable from this concept (Dworkin 1977). However, Dworkin's arguments have been criticised as legal imperialism (Hunt 1992). Dworkin's theory is presented in terms of formal rights and not substantive rights and rights therefore become 'commodities' that need to be hoarded (Hutchinson 1992). There is a lack of attention to substantive inequalities and this, in part, legitimises the continuation of socio-economic inequalities. Thus structural forces, such as class and gender, through which other forces of power are exercised on individuals, together with their relationship with state power, are largely ignored (Munzer 1990, Edgeworth 1992).

The possibility of applying Rawls' theory to health care has been explored by Pogge (1989) and Daniels (1985). Pogge argues that by extending Rawls' theory to health care there should be *formal* equality of medical opportunity. For Pogge, *fair* equality of medical opportunity is concerned with the distribution of *health:* that is the distribution of medical care relative to medical needs (he assumes that medical needs occur naturally). His approach is that social systems are not unjust if medical needs are unmet. Injustices arise if people are denied access and find that their needs are not being met whilst those of people with comparable needs are. Daniels (1985) clearly argues that health care should be governed by the principle of justice guaranteeing fair equality of opportunity.

if an acceptable general theory of distributive justice requires us to guarantee fair equality of opportunity, then a principle for the distribution of health-care seems to follow. (Daniels 1985, p. 86)

He attempts to do this by stating that within the framework of Rawls' theory, health care should be a background institution that ensures equality of opportunity. This should not be taken to mean that the health care system can be considered in isolation from the rest of society, for such an approach can give the illusion of equality within the system when it is in fact surrounded by a sea of inequality. As Seedhouse says:

Equal access to health services makes sense only if 'equal access for equal need' has been first applied to other areas of life so as to truly make illness/disease/sickness a matter of misfortune rather than something which could have been avoided given more general egalitarian planning. (Seedhouse 1994, p. 80)

Daniels' approach is important in that his definition of equity as equality of opportunity for equal need is a principle that operates independently of Rawls' theory. Daniels' approach has a clear and significant concern for needs and the extent to which individuals can derive rights from their needs. Daniels argues that the normal opportunity range (NOR) in any given society will be the range of life plans that reasonable persons will construct. Now this range will vary in distribution according to the society (i.e. it is relative) but normal species functioning acts as a clear parameter to allow us to define the normal opportunity range. Some diseases will have more serious effects on the NOR than others but because NORs are relative (between societies) the impact of the same diseases will be different between societies. Therefore if we work on the principle of impairment of opportunity then the social effects of diseases will be important. Within a society the NOR is abstracted from effective opportunity, that is individual sub sets of NOR. Impairment of NOR is a crude measure of the relative importance of society's health care needs. In this sense Daniels deals in aggregates at the macro level and clearly recognises that these may differ from individual perceptions of the good.

The question that needs to be addressed is how is it possible to measure impairment and its effects on the NOR. Should we use a full range satisfaction scale or a truncated scale of well being?[12] Rawls argues for a truncated scale rather than a satisfaction scale on the basis that a satisfaction scale commits us to an unacceptable view of persons as 'containers' for satisfaction. This is an important point, for a further danger is that individuals are treated as mere foci for measurement rather than moral agents. Just distributions of health care resources therefore have to be based on shared understandings of the relationship between needs, disability and normal opportunity. This presents problems in that (as we have already seen) these are disputed concepts and even where there is no dispute we must be wary of ways in which structural forces act to distort understandings.

A minimal criterion for justice

It is clear from our discussion so far that the concept of justice is problematic and attempts to develop liberal theories of justice are open to charges of naiveté towards the operation of power in society. Habermas offers a universal but minimal criterion for justice as a way through this morass (White 1988). The justice of normative claims can be assessed by universal procedural criteria but this does not amount to specifying a set of universal principles on which justice is based. For Habermas, a universal account of justice is only possible through his conception of communicative action (Habermas 1990). Agreement over a proposed norm is only legitimate if it is based on a communicative discourse involving all those affected by the norm. Norms are the focus for legitimising the satisfaction of 'human interests' or 'needs'. This does not mean that Habermas accepts the notion of universal basic needs. Needs are culturally variable and specific to societies in that they are a function of what each society believes is necessary for the flourishing of human life. The concept of objective universal needs has been undermined by arguments about the fragmentation of modern society and the elevation of consumption as means of defining the 'self'. Marxists can also see needs as socially relative, arguing that within capitalist societies the structure of needs is specific to capitalism (Soper 1981, Geras 1983). Any attempt to apply needs, as defined by modern capitalist society, in some objective universal sense to other societies, is seen as cultural imperialism. The importance of this argument is seen in attempts by those in power to use definitions of needs to legitimise their own wants. In response to this it is argued that needs are legitimate and objective only when they are determined by specific oppressed groups (Walzer 1983).

Ethnomethodological arguments link into this debate in that they question any attempt to impose explanations of social phenomena in one group by another group. The only way of coping with this is to *describe* the different subjective notions of need that are employed in social contexts. This view firmly rejects a universal objective notion of need seeing it instead as a dynamic social construct. These arguments are particularly relevant to health care because attempts to define health care needs can be criticised in the sense that they can only reflect professional perspectives and professional ideology. Against such a backdrop any attempt to define health care needs is always open to criticisms of having a dual role of subjugating the individual or group being assessed to the needs of the system or professional interests within the system, whilst simultaneously constructing a picture of what that individual or group 'needs'.

However there are problems with the relativist position. How can we be sure that definitions of need within an oppressed group will not contain definitions that are oppressing people within the group? Arguments about fragmentation and cultural imperialism are contradictory in that they do accept that need exists but it is argued that only the group in question can assess them. If you are oppressed then there must be some standard by means of which your suffering is measured otherwise how could either you or anyone else know you are being oppressed. Sexism and racism can only be bad if we have a notion of what is good or bad as a reference point. Every group, even an oppressed group, has powerful vested interests leading it. If we accept that this happens then the search for standards external to any group to evaluate their moral standing is valid. But if we are to address the criticism that such standards involve cultural imperialism, we will need a coherent theory to inform them so that the distortions of need that are an inherent part of modern capitalist society can be avoided. Our search must be for a framework for discussing needs, particularly intermediate needs and their satisfiers, in an open and fair manner which allows these needs to change and develop in response to this open and fair debate. However, the capacity of the language of need to act as a means of social control should not be forgotten in the rush to demonstrate agreement (Fraser 1989). Striving for a better understanding of needs, through communicative practices, does not entail specifying the basic needs everyone has in a 'good society', for such a project ignores the requirement of reciprocity (since some potential voices will not be given a fair hearing). It is the requirement of reciprocity that is at the heart of Habermas' criticism of Rawls' theory of justice. Persons in the original position are contracting on the basis of a pre-defined set of primary goods, (liberty, opportunity, wealth and income). These create a bias towards a particular type of society. Rawls seems to recognise this when he accepts that his version of justice is valid only for members of 'modern democratic societies' (Rawls 1980). The communicative ethics proposed by Habermas illuminates the road towards fair procedures for judging normative claims. Such an ethics requires that actors engaged in discourse be flexible, critical and willing to change their view of needs in response to the discourse. The importance of this for health care can be found in the dilemmas arising from those attempts, discussed so far, to extend Rawls' theory of justice to cover health care. Doyal and Gough argue that the relationship between harm and impaired social participation is fundamental to the identification of need. In order that social participation is optimised then impairment has to be minimised. This is true whether impairment is acquired genetically or otherwise. Health care is a social good that operates to minimise levels of impairment and disability. If health care is to be allocated in a just and equitable manner then policy must be grounded in shared understandings of what is necessary for social participation, based on procedures that rely on communicative discourses. It is here that they base the procedural part of their theory on Habermas' communicative ethics. This in turn has implications for any understanding of rights to health care.

Rights to health care

No one has the right to a specific treatment under the NHS. Health Authorities are only required to have regard to the health needs of the population. To say that an individual has a right to something implies that someone else has an obligation in respect of that right. In other words rights entail duties (Waldron 1984). If we accept that health is a fundamental prerequisite for individuals to participate fully in society then expecting people to be good citizens contains an implicit commitment to ensure that they achieve optimum levels of health (Montgomery 1992).

Public perceptions of the NHS are based on the concept of universal access at the point of need and the notion of a fundamental right to health care has very strong support. But the relationship between the public's concept of the right to health care, the historical background to such rights and their relationship with the concept of equity are extremely complex. Increasing societal pressures on individuals to take responsibility for their health are linked to the concept of an automatic right to receive care being questioned and proscribed (ten Have and Loughlin 1994). If there is support among the general population for the right to free health care then this has implications for any attempt to ration by means of restricting treatments. Equally, if health is a basic human need that entails rights and responsibilities, the health care system cannot be examined in isolation from other demands on society. In this sense it would be immoral to ration health care when resources are being expended on areas which do not provide for basic human needs in the same way. The problem is that of reconciling rights, needs and resources against a backdrop of scarce resources and misuse of resources. Under conditions of scarcity, needs cannot automatically entail rights (Plant 1992). The argument that someone has a right to demand health care from the state contains an implicit requirement that this demand is given a priority. This is not to say that a right is absolute for there may be other more pressing policy considerations. In contrast to this, it could be argued that whilst resources are still being used inappropriately then the relationship between need and rights has enough moral force to make any rationing of satisfiers of basic needs untenable. The link between health needs (based on the minimisation of impairment and disability) and rights lies in the expectation that individuals meet the duties of citizenship. If these duties are to be met then individuals have a right to basic need satisfaction to enable them to fulfil their duties. If rationing is to be made explicit then the relationship between needs and rights also has to be made explicit. If debates about health needs are to be democratic then they have to be embedded in a process that strives for a shared understanding of needs and the rights that the needs, so identified, entail.

Conclusion

This chapter has looked at the theoretical debates concerning health care needs, justice and rights to health care. The extent to which health care needs can be considered objective and measurable has been discussed in the light of different theories and Doyal and Gough's theory has been examined as a possible avenue for treating health care as an intermediate need. The problem of how the health care system can operate in a just manner has been considered and I have shown that the way we arrive at a view of a just health care system is dependent on the ways in which we define needs. This in turn has repercussions for our understanding of rights to health care. In order to address these issues Doyal and Gough have constructed a theory of human need that has a substantive part which sets out the arguments for basic needs and a procedural part setting out a framework for coming to agreement about how needs are to be met and how they are to be prioritised. This procedural framework uses Habermas' communicative ethics as a basis. Any attempt to situate this theory within a practical policy framework must however address the capacity of power and vested interests to distort debates concerning needs and rights. In this book I use the example of rationing treatments for End Stage Renal Failure in the UK as a backdrop to my discussions. If we are to gain an understanding of how such rationing policies come about, how they are legitimised, perpetuated and challenged, then we need to consider the relationship between health policy, health needs and the operation of power. In the next chapter I consider the ways in which Habermas' communicative ethics can bring a critical perspective to this relationship.

Notes

1   I view the term 'New Right' as encompassing libertarians and neo-conservatives. It is however important to distinguish between the two because the former are committed to free market policies on the basis of theories of personal freedom whilst the latter support free markets because of their presumed link with traditional values, the family and the disciplining force of respect for authority. These two approaches bring different perspectives to bear on needs: on the one hand from a commitment to personal freedom and on the other from a commitment to social policies based on 'moral standards'. The impact of New Right thinking on health policy in the UK has stemmed from the way in which these two separate streams of thought were mixed together to form the drive to expose the NHS to the disciplining effects of the market under Thatcherism.

2   Health economics is the application of the discipline of economics to the topic of health care (Mooney 1986 p. 5). It brings to health care the question of choosing between competing alternatives for action within the limits of scarce resources. The goal of health economics therefore is efficiency. Within these parameters however there is plenty of scope for health economists to develop different approaches to their discipline.

3   Doyal and Gough define the 'optimum' at two levels; the participatory optimum and critical optimum. The first refers to levels of health and autonomy such that individuals can choose the activities in which they will take part within their culture. The second refers to levels of health and autonomy such that individuals can question their form of life and participate in political processes that allow them to be critical and change cultures. In neither case does optimum imply maximum. (Doyal and Gough 1991, p. 160)

4   It is important to clarify the meaning of terms like 'satiable' and 'basic' in relation to needs. The term basic needs implies a narrow range of needs that are essential for human functioning. A satiable need implies a need that can be fully satiated by the resources available to society. A satisfiable need may or may not be fully satiated and can be met either by the provision of a specific satisfier or by manipulating the need itself.

5   Marginal analysis starts from the existing pattern of expenditure of resources and considers the effect of small changes to that pattern.

6   The 'agency relationship' refers to the way in which the doctor acts as the agent of the ill-informed patient.

7   This linking of Borges' story to a discussion of justice is taken from Beauchamp and Childress (1989).

8   The debate concerning QALYs has also considered the equity of policies based on SAVEs and HYEs (Saved young lives and Healthy Years Equivalents), (Meherez and Gafni 1989, Buckingham 1993).

9   At the level of society QALYs could result in weak and vulnerable groups being denied treatment precisely because they are weak and vulnerable and thus unable to achieve good QALY scores.

10 Horizontal equity refers to the equal treatment of people in equal states and vertical equity refers to the unequal treatment of people in unequal states.

11 Rawls argues that rational contractors in a fair bargaining situation behind a 'veil of ignorance' would accept the following principles of justice :

    (I)   The principle of equal liberty

    (IIa)   The difference principle
                  (The difference principle permits inequalities in the distribution of social-economic goods only if they benefit everyone especially the least advantaged)

    (IIb)   The principle of fair equality of opportunity

The principle of equal liberty has absolute priority over other principles and must be satisfied before these are considered. Moreover the principle of fair equality of opportunity has priority over the difference principle.

12 A full range satisfaction scale considers the complete range of an individuals' needs and preferences. A truncated scale is a selective scale which excludes some preferences and focuses on the things we claim to need (see Daniels 1985 pp. 24-25).

3 Health policy: a critical perspective

Every point of view, every kind of knowledge and every kind of experience is limited and ignorant. (Delmore Schwartz 1959, Summer Knowledge: author's note)

My discussion so far has drawn on Doyal and Gough's theory of human need as a basis for my critique of various approaches to health care needs. At the same time I have drawn attention to certain tensions within Doyal and Gough's own project that stem from an attempt to situate their theory in a practical policy framework. In order to better understand these tensions therefore it is necessary to consider the various paradigms of health policy that are available to us and how these can form the basis for a practical understanding of health care needs in relation to policy. If, as Doyal and Gough argue, it is possible to construct a basis for discussing human needs from Habermas' communicative ethics, then we must be confident that such an ethics, placed in the context of the health care system, is capable of operating despite the tensions and conflicts that exist within that system. This in turn requires an understanding of the operation of power in the system.

I begin this chapter by looking at the history of policy explanations in the NHS, concentrating on four major theoretical perspectives; neo-pluralist, public choice, neo-elitist and neo-Marxist. I move on to examine the development of markets in health care; considering the structure of markets and the extent to which contracts for health services can be based on assessments of needs. I consider the implications of each theoretical perspective for an understanding of health care needs. I then examine theories of power in relation to the NHS, highlighting the importance of an understanding of the operation of power for my analysis of health policy.

Subsequently I outline the relevance of Habermas' communicative ethics to the debates concerning power. Finally I set out how a Habermasian framework can be used as part of an analysis of policy making. I will explore the problems that stem from the use of idealised states to criticise and at the same time create a practical state of affairs.

Paradigms of health policy: the history of policy explanations

During the 1960s and early 1970s a set of shared policy views on health and welfare was developed, reflecting the consensus politics of the time (Harrison et al 1990). At a public level this consensus was reflected in popular support for the NHS (Taylor-Gooby 1985, Klein 1983) whose durability has been evidenced in recent debates on the resourcing and reorganisation of the NHS. Health policy was increasingly explained by incrementalist models as opposed to rational comprehensive models of the system (Lindblom 1959, 1979). The incremental analysis stood in direct opposition to any attempt at developing a grand theory. Its attractions were numerous. The policy process was described as one of 'partisan mutual adjustment' between various actors in the system. The actors in this adjustment process were the medical profession, consumers, lay representatives and managers all of whom played different roles and occupied different partitions of power. These actors were caricatured as being powerful (Doctors), weak (lay members and consumers) and reactive (managers).

This paradigm provided elegant descriptions of policy changes in the sixties and seventies and still has powerful explanatory powers when applied to local area levels of health management (DHAs and trusts) (Harrison et al 1990). The theory failed to describe adequately policy processes at the level of central government and, because of its relativist position, was open to the charge that it could not distinguish between small and large changes. In other words it could not provide a way of telling when an incremental shift becomes a radical shift. This critique became increasingly relevant during the 1980s as Conservative governments set out to reform the structure of the NHS. Incrementalism's failure to provide a comprehensive explanation of policy changes is linked to its superficial treatment of power relationships.

Theories of distributive power have been applied increasingly to the health policy field. Allsop (1984) discusses theories of professional dominance, political economy, Marxism and the New Right as explanatory accounts of health policy. Similarly Ham (1985) discusses three theoretical approaches (Marxist, pluralist and structuralist) and suggests that of themselves they provide incomplete accounts but taken together have considerable potential

41

for policy analysis. Harrison et al (1990) consider four theories in the light of the NHS reforms; neo-pluralism, public choice theory, neo-elitism and neo-Marxism. It is these theories that I turn to as a starting point for my own analysis of policy.

Neo-pluralism

Classic pluralism saw power as being widely distributed within society, with negotiation taking place between groups through a bargaining process that had the state as a focus. Neo-pluralism gives greater emphasis to the unequal nature of relations in this process. This refinement denies the state complete neutrality in the bargaining process. The advance made by neo-pluralists is seen in their acceptance of the role of big business and capital in the power game. The theory does not however deal with structural constraints (e.g. demographic change) and their effect on decisions. With respect to the NHS reforms Harrison et al (1990) argue that neo-pluralism does not explain policy changes. Government is clearly not a referee between competing interests, and has taken an active and centralised approach to directing policy, whilst lobbying, although energetic and sometimes successful at local level, has not been decisive in influencing broad policy decisions. The neo-pluralist account of policy has strengths in explaining the inability of the system to address health care needs. If policy is based on negotiation, with the state playing a fulcrum role, then a neo-pluralist argument could suggest that the language of needs has developed to form the lynch pin of negotiation. In this sense an appeal to needs based policy is the 'appeal in the last resort' of a semi-codified language of negotiation. Unfortunately within the constraints of neo-pluralist theory this argument fails to explain the role of the Department of Health in trying to develop resource allocation policies that are based on an assessment of health care needs.

Public choice theory

At the heart of public choice theory is the classical economic belief in the utility maximising individual, the moral superiority of markets and the threat that welfarism represents to liberty. However, the quality of the arguments supporting this view tend to vary considerably. Some seem to think it sufficient to argue that the market, through the price mechanism, involves voluntary exchanges of goods and services between individuals, (Friedman and Friedman 1980). But this analysis is too simplistic and relies on a naive view of the price mechanism that fails to situate it within institutional conditions. According to Hindess (1987):

> Friedman's social analysis reduces to three interacting
> elements: human individuals making choices, governments
> interfering, and chance. (p. 126)

Hayek, on the other hand, offers a more challenging theory that has had considerable implications for debates on welfare provision and social policy, (Hayek 1944). Hayek sets up an argument against central planning and in favour of the market because the former cannot gather together sufficient knowledge about the required social order in the same way that the later does through market mechanisms. In addition to this Hayek argues that central planning is dangerous because it leads to coercion by the state and sets limits to freedom. This view of the welfare state as a coercive force has been extremely influential in the development of a public choice theory approach to welfare policy and to health policy. Niskanen (1971) is one who argued that public sector bureaucracies tend to over-supply services because managers try to maximise their own utility through maximising their own budgets. In this way the public choice theorists have been able to present themselves as arguing against a system that promotes professional interests at the expense of human needs. However, contradictions in their arguments can be found in simultaneous attempts to deny basic needs and show that the welfare state fails to meet needs (Goodin 1988).

Public choice theory does not adequately explain developments of health policy even within the context of a government whose ideology has been directed by such thinking. The 'inefficient' central planning of 1970s welfarism for example, failed to result in an oversupply of health care. Indeed, in comparison to other countries, the NHS has been singularly successful in controlling costs and restricting funding within capped budgets. In light of this it is worth questioning whether the NHS reforms were the result of policy making led by public choice theorists. Perhaps the public choice arguments are more an attempt to rationalise in retrospect those actions already decided upon. In elevating the price mechanism and consumer sovereignty to an idealised status, public choice theorists are dismissive of human 'needs'. Needs per se are only discussed in terms of a minimum set of basic necessities. Any attempt to plan welfare services on the basis of need is seen as inefficient and patronising at best and coercive at its worst. For a government whose ideology was so clearly directed by public choice thinking therefore, a health care system that gives responsibility to its officers to assess health care needs would seem somewhat of a contradiction. It is difficult to marry loyalty to the notion of consumer sovereignty with the existence of a professional cadre of needs assessors. The quasi-market in health care was dressed up in the rhetoric of consumer choice and patient participation. It is here that appeals to the 'language of need' have to be set in context, and questions have to be asked of the commitments being made to a health care system that in principle allocates resources according to an assessment of need. Specifically, it is important to ask whether this aspect of the reforms represented a three way compromise between free market theorising, the imperatives of state bureaucracy and the demands of professional dominant interests.

Neo-elitism

Neo-elitism argues that power is concentrated in the hands of elites. These elites may conflict with one another but in the main they co-operate to prevent mass participation. Liberal corporatism, is a recent development of neo-elitism which sees the state offering favours and status to a few select groups in return for their moderating influence (Schmitter 1974). The medical profession is a clear candidate for interpretation as one of these favoured groups. However, the role of the medical profession in opposing the NHS reforms does not correspond with this view of health policy (Harrison et al 1992).

Structural interest theory, (Alford 1975), is a brand of neo-elite theory that allows for competition between elites. Alford defined interests by their relationship with the principles by which institutions operate. He identified three interest groups:

'dominant interests' --- Doctors
'challenging interest' --- Managers (corporate rationalisers)
'repressed interests' --- Community groups and population groups

The usefulness of this approach is that it deals with the policy processes that go on between and within organisations. Its weakness is that it cannot analyse economic and technological changes very well. Alford's theories give insight and understanding into the ability of hospital consultants to maintain control over their working practices. The impact of national policies on their main areas of interest are minimised by means of strategies of avoidance. Seen in the light of neo-elite theory the 1984 general management reforms and *Working for Patients* therefore seem to be attempts to give management the power and momentum to challenge medical elites. The period of post-war consensus has been replaced by policies that emphasise the role of management (corporate rationalisers), who are being encouraged by means of incentives and the direction of policy to challenge medical interests.

The implications of Alford's theories of structural interests for a theory of health care needs can be found in the extent to which these structural interests take needs seriously. The idea that the language of need is used as a negotiating instrument is important here. In addition to this, Alford's theory

44

sheds light on the extent to which different definitions of need are used by these structural interests as they compete. At a simple level the 'dominant interest groups' (physicians) appeal to clinical definitions of need, the corporate rationalisers (management) tend to adopt an economic approach to need, whilst the 'repressed interests' tend to present a 'community' based notion of need. Such tendencies can be seen in the debates in the review group set out in this book (see later) in the concerns of the physicians on the group for an epidemiological analysis of needs and the managers concerns for the relationship between needs and contracting, both of which can be contrasted with patient group concerns for the survival of their local hospitals. The relationship between the different groups was more complex than this suggests and there was 'cross-fertilisation' between the beliefs of these different structural interests. Nevertheless the analysis is useful in providing an understanding of how confusion arises concerning needs based policies and the extent to which rights and duties can be ascribed to individual needs.

Neo-Marxism and the New Left

Orthodox Marxism presented a mechanistic approach to social policy whereby in the struggle between capital and labour the state was portrayed as the instrument of the capitalist class. Neo-Marxism has developed this analysis so that the class structure is given a more complex structural analysis. Elites are not seen as the result of a deterministic economic/social process but are related to the underlying class structure. The consequence of neo-Marxist analysis for social policy is that the state is no longer seen as the tool of the capitalist state but instead the welfare state is given a duality that sees it at one level as part of the functional requirements of capitalism and at another level as an achievement resulting from working class struggle. In this sense the welfare state is seen as a battleground (Poulantzas 1978). This 'paradox' of welfare is best summed up by Gough (1979):

> once universal suffrage and the other major liberal rights are established , this provides a crucial channel through which to obtain welfare improvements. Indeed, welfare becomes a means of integrating the enfranchised working class within the capitalist system and of obtaining certain concessions from the organised labour movement (Gough 1979, pp. 60-61-quoted in Hindess 1987)

Neo-Marxists still see the liberal state as being unable to cope with the plurality of demands made of it (Offe 1985). Within this critique the welfare state, and the NHS as part of it, maintains inequalities. These arguments

45

have echoes in the work of Barr (1987) who argues that the welfare state operates as an efficiency device.

The neo-Marxist approach sets out three categories of welfare expenditure; social expenses to maintain order (police), social investment (supporting the process of capital accumulation e.g. transport and energy) and social consumption (health and welfare to maintain the workforce and to 'legitimate' the system). Capital interests are divided between industrial capital and financial capital and between local capital and international capital. With respect to health care policy these arguments formulate an extremely powerful analysis providing explanatory insights on the formulation of the NHS, episodes such as CBI lobbying for reductions in NHS workforce and the so called 'crisis of welfare' in the 1980s and 1990s. The significant contribution of the Marxist analysis is to be found in the account of the crisis of legitimacy. The capitalist system, in theory, should only invest in the welfare state up to the point where it optimises legitimacy.

The relationship of neo-Marxist theory to health policy and health care needs seems to be focused on the interpretation of the pursuit by the state of a policy based on an assessment of needs. The significant factor in this relationship is that health policy placed the responsibility of identifying needs and allocating resources in the hands of Purchasing Authorities in the role of 'champions of the people'. Purchasers acted as a buffer between central government and the residents they serve. This allowed the centralisation of state power and the devolution of responsibility to occur simultaneously leading to concerns about accountability within the system. Indeed, some commentators have argued that this led to Stalinist tendencies in the NHS (Craft 1994). The authoritarian roles of surveillance, monitoring, assessing needs and reporting to central government sit uneasily with any attempt to empower and involve local populations in decision making. The conflicts that arise from this are manifested in part through the language of need. As far as measuring health care needs are concerned, Marxists see attempts at introducing cost-efficiency, performance indicators, savings etc. as means to secure greater output (legitimacy) for less input.

Quasi-markets in health care

The Thatcher government had made significant changes to the management of the health service following the Griffiths report (Griffiths 1983). However, the concept of a universal health system financed from taxation remained largely intact between 1979 and 1987. Nevertheless, it was clear that the government was searching for more radical ways of reforming the NHS and the critique of the British system by the American economist Alain Enthoven (1985) and the solutions he offered in terms of internal markets finally led a review of the financing and organisation of health care in Britain and ultimately to *Working for Patients* (DoH 1989a). *Working for Patients* created a separation between purchasers of health services (DHAs, FHSAs and GP fundholders) and providers of health services (NHS trusts and Directly Managed Units, private and voluntary sector providers). Purchasers were given an annual budget, in the case of Health Authorities this was calculated according to allocative formulas based on population size, age and proxies for morbidity. In the case of GP fundholders this was based on historical patterns of service use. In both cases they were required to spend this money according to the needs of their populations. In general the providers provided levels of service in return for an agreed sum and the focus for this agreement was the contract for health care. Enthoven's critique of the NHS paid tribute to the success of the system in containing costs, to the strength of primary care and to the economies of scale arising from the concentration of specialties. He argued however that the system was too rigid, over centralised and contained perverse incentives. These weaknesses resulted in inefficiencies, lack of innovation, poor accountability and lack of responsiveness to the consumer of health services. Enthoven proposed the creation of a demand side (purchasers of health care) that was separate from the supply side (providers of health care) to create the necessary conditions for markets to operate (Enthoven 1991). The terms internal markets, quasi-markets and managed markets have been used to describe such a system. Although these terms can be used interchangeably, I have settled on the term quasi-markets to describe the system as it existed in the NHS.

It is tempting to view Enthoven's critique as the manifestation of attacks on the NHS by the Right but we should not forget that quasi-markets had also been advocated by some writers on the political left (Young 1989). Quasi-markets have also played a significant role in post-Fordist developments of capitalist organisation where centralised bureaucracies have decentralised by means of contracting out (Harvey 1989). Quasi-markets could never result in the introduction of 'the market' to the NHS either in its pure, abstract sense or in the sense of markets for goods and services in the high street. This is because quasi-markets are by definition different in nature to ideal markets as well as the imperfect markets of the private sector. On the demand side the power of the consumer is not expressed in terms of individual ability to pay but in terms of budgetary allocations or vouchers. The agent for the expression of this power is a central government bureaucracy or a third party such as a GP fundholder. On the supply side the motives of suppliers may not be profit maximisation and the ownership of assets is often blurred. These factors combine to make quasi-markets operate differently to ordinary markets and produce a complex set of problems and weaknesses many of which Enthoven failed to highlight.

These weaknesses cast doubt on the ability of the system to meet the promised objectives of increased efficiency and improved responsiveness.

Contracting and quasi-markets

Immediately following the publication of *Working for Patients* the NHS Management Executive set itself the task of producing a set of operational principles for contracting in the new system. These principles were set out in September 1989 and they outlined a framework for agreeing general principles, for negotiating contracts, monitoring contracts and settling disputes (DoH 1989b). Early guidance covered such matters as the type of contracts, their duration, quality, the setting of prices, management responsibilities and the establishment of patient residency for the purposes of billing. As time went on however, guidance became increasingly concerned with ways in which the assessment of population need could be used as a basis for contracts. This culminated in a three pronged approach to needs assessment as a basis for the contracting process (DoH 1990, DoH 1991). The cautious approach of the Central Management Executive towards the introduction of free markets in the first year of contracting is significant in that it betrayed a sense of uncertainty and a need to maintain the status quo. The key phrase at this time was 'steady state' and it highlighted a tension between a policy that called for more devolved decision making and fear of what markets could do to the system if they were allowed to operate freely. These tensions were rationalised by analysts who saw that if markets were to be managed then this required a deeper understanding of the nature of quasi-markets than had hitherto been the case (Roberts 1993).

Market structures

The idealised market structure is one where there are many providers on the supply side and many purchasers on the demand side resulting in a competitive environment. Price in such a market should be responsive to demand and supply. Although the New Right place their faith in the capacity of markets to deliver health care more efficiently, this faith was based on limited evidence (Glaser 1993). Indeed the evidence in the UK has been largely contradictory (Light and May 1993). It is useful to distinguish between market imperfections in general which can be found at all levels of the system and imperfection of health care markets in particular. Health care markets are inherently imperfect because they offer a multiplicity of opportunities for doctors and managers to collude, to manipulate markets, to segment markets and shift costs (Light 1993). On top of this, health care markets are complicated by reason of the product involved (health care and ultimately health) being so difficult to define. The relationship between purchaser, provider and consumer is complex because their roles are often blurred with purchasers relying on providers to specify the goods and services being bought whilst consumers place both providers and purchasers in a position of trust in terms of the appropriateness, quality and price of the goods they receive. Information on products is difficult to interpret and time consuming to collect and this makes 'shopping around' for the best service almost impossible for consumers who often do not want to do this because they are already ill. The location of providers, particularly in rural areas means that conditions necessary for choice do not exist, thus monopoly markets operate. Finally poor quality providers are protected from the possibility of exit from the market and can operate at low levels of capacity whilst the better providers are overburdened with excess activity.

This is a far cry from the notion of 'contestability' (Baumol et al 1982) where the threat of new entrants into the market is believed to instil competitive discipline. If we consider the possibility of market segmentation however, the concept of contestability does have some force. For highly specialised treatments such as transplantation and some forms of cancer therapy the economies of scale involved make monopoly supply attractive and diminish contestability. For treatments such as renal dialysis however, contestability is much more of a reality as increasingly the major service determinant is patient convenience. Distinguishing between fixed costs (costs that remain until activity ceases) and sunk costs (costs that continue beyond cessation of activity) is useful because they influence the risk associated with contestability. Providers with large sunk costs have more to lose if their contracts are terminated or diminished in any way. Asset specificity, the extent to which assets can be redeployed, has similar consequences. It is unclear whether the annual cycle of contracting in the health service was sufficiently flexible to accommodate the risks involved in such market structures (Roberts 1993). In trying to shift some of the risks involved on to the purchasers, franchise type arrangements, where providers lease capital assets from the purchasers, became a real possibility. The potential of this for renal services was considerable as satellite dialysis units and their equipment could be quickly set up by purchasers in geographically accessible areas and then contracts agreed with providers to provide a service from those units. Where the risks of entering into contracts were high however, close relationships between purchasers and providers developed to such an extent that institutional loyalties became entrenched and contracting evolved according to an increasingly specialised language. These close relationships could be interpreted as having positive or negative repercussions for the ultimate consumer of services. A specialised language evolved where the explanations, terms and definitions used as a basis for contracts became more intelligible for those involved in the contracting process and less understandable for those outside this process.

The way quasi-markets function is dependent on the nature of transaction costs and the extent of uncertainty. Transaction costs can be divided into *ex ante* exchange (costs incurred in drafting and negotiating contracts) and *ex post* exchange (costs incurred in monitoring outcomes and ensuring compliance) (Williamson 1975). The tendency is that high *ex ante* costs lead to lower *ex post* costs and low *ex ante* costs lead to higher *ex post* costs. Arguments against the introduction of markets highlighted low transaction costs in the system before the reforms. The global shift towards decentralisation, flatter organisations and other aspects of post-Fordist forms of production may, on the other hand, reflect the capacity of new information technologies to reduce transaction costs. Nevertheless, the setting up of quasi-markets in the health service involved a considerable degree of investment in new technologies and management personnel reflecting a tendency toward higher transaction costs.

Uncertainty is a feature of markets that can make it difficult for purchasers and providers to engage in forward planning. This tendency is compounded by the difficulties involved in processing the complex pools of information that comprise market signals. This is the bounded rationality that Williamson (1975) refers to and in the face of the uncertainties involved, organisations construct bureaucracies and hierarchical structures to cope with such an environment. The role of contracts as mechanisms that are designed to minimise uncertainty and risk is crucial. It is through the need to enforce and monitor contractual obligations that purchasers and providers; a) incur increasing transaction costs and b) concentrate their contracting energies.

The motivation of actors involved in the contracting process is rarely clear cut. Providers are not profit maximisers and their actions are often motivated by the desire for kudos and to protect budgets. The role of purchasers is also unclear in that the 'champions of the people' often find the interests of consumers, the need to preserve good relations with providers and their own long term interests, in conflict. The position and motives of purchasers are significant in relation to the assessment of the needs of consumers. Whereas in conventional markets the consumption of goods is determined by the ability to pay, quasi-markets place a third party between the consumer and the providers and access to goods and services is dependent on the need criteria of the third party purchaser (often using provider advice as a guide). It has been argued that quasi-markets establish:

> a correspondence between need and consumption. Where
> this correspondence is achieved, the quasi-market will meet
> the criteria of equity in the use of services. (Bartlett and
> Harrison 1993, p. 32)

Now this is a considerable claim on behalf of quasi-markets and its validity is dependent to a large extent on the meaning of need in this context and the absence of 'cream skimming', that is the ability of providers to discriminate against high cost users. These factors cause confusion concerning the question of what contracts can deliver. Quasi-markets could create incentives for increased efficiency and for reducing costs. On the other hand where the risks are high then this could lead to increasing costs and opportunism leading to reductions in quality and productive efficiency.

Insufficient knowledge and information to monitor contracts leaves purchasers in the position of having to trust providers as far as the levels and quality of services are concerned. Opportunistic behaviour becomes more likely in such circumstances. This can present itself as a form of moral hazard, where providers provide a lower quality service than is specified in the contract, and where information that places the provider in a bad light is concealed from the purchaser. Cream skimming is also a danger in such circumstances. In the NHS the response to the possibility of such opportunistic behaviour was to look to accreditation and registration systems and to rely on the role of professional ethics in maintaining a baseline of treatment according to clinical need. The pressures that quasi-markets brought to bear on physician behaviour when budgets were capped should not be underestimated however, and this led Roberts to write in 1993:

> Treatments according to medical need and no other criteria appears less and less likely to guide the ethics of medical practice. (Roberts 1993, p. 308)

Clearly the market in the form of the Purchaser/Provider split was not designed as a means of injecting more money into the system from central funds, rather it was a mechanism for improving efficiency. One of the ways the market addressed efficiency considerations was by bringing scarcity of resources into sharp focus. This is because the limited budgets of Purchasing Authorities were now applicable to defined populations. The NHS has always been subject to scarcity but purchasing, in theory at least, offered new ways of addressing the problem:

1   By challenging 'provider capture' - the way resources have gravitated towards traditional areas of professional interest; purchasing could act as a lever for allocating resources towards priority areas thus breaking away from historical patterns.

2   It presented opportunities to reflect the views of local people. Purchasing Authorities were encouraged to develop the role of 'champion of the people'.

3   Purchasers were concerned to buy services that are cost-effective. The extent to which purchasing offered 'value for money' was therefore a crucial strand in arguments in its favour.

However, purchasing either created or highlighted a number of dilemmas (Heginbotham et al 1992). These included the balance between expert and lay opinion, the conflict between individual need and institutional response, the resourcing of acute versus community services, prevention versus intervention, weighing the quality of life against saving life itself and the priority given to maintaining a balance of services across all care groups against priorities within care groups. Most of these dilemmas existed before quasi-markets but purchasing seemed to bring them into a sharper light.

Purchasing was seen by some as ethically good because it forced rationing decisions out into the open (Harrison 1991). However, there was a considerable gap between the rhetoric of democratic accountability and the extent to which communities became involved in reality. Which communities should be consulted, how could complex issues be presented to the public in a meaningful way (Bowling 1993)? Were Purchasers 'champions of the people', or were they engaging in social control (Jones 1992)? Purchasing seemed therefore to represent a change in the balance of power. The extent to which power relationships shifted in reality was unclear (Harrison et al 1992). The policy implications of these shifts in spheres of influence can only be grasped if we consider theories of power in the NHS.

Theories of power in the NHS

The analysis of power in organisations can be traced to Weber's work on bureaucracies which focused on power operating on hierarchical levels (Giddens 1971). This approach was expanded by Lukes (1974) to include the operation of control over individuals. Attempts have also been made to account for the way structural factors affect policy discussions through individual policy actors (Harrison et al 1990).

Power operates at a number of levels. The 'first face' of power presents itself as open conflict whereupon an individual or group submits to the demands made by others through the open operation of power. The 'second face' of power operates through the manipulation of processes and institutions by the powerful to ensure that their preferred interests are addressed and issues that challenge those interests are suppressed (Ham and Hill 1984). This can be achieved either through direct action taken by the powerful or by subordinate groups deciding not to raise the issue because

52

they feel that it's 'not worth it'. In this way the powerful are able to preserve and even advance their interests without engaging in open conflict (Bachrach and Baratz 1970). The third face of power operates invisibly by stimulating, shaping and swaying the desires and wants of others. In this way the powerful are not only able to maintain their authority but also gain legitimacy in the eyes of those they dominate (Lukes 1974). This third face of power presents problems for policy analysts because of its invisibility, for how is one to analyse something that by definition lies hidden from view? The invisibility of the third face of power does not however mean that it is undetectable nor is it immune from critical analysis.

Within the NHS, power operates at all of the levels discussed above. Attempts by the conservative government to diminish trade union strength during the 1980s seem to have operated in tandem with a strategy to increase control over the NHS structure through the introduction of general management. The first and second faces of power were clearly at work in this process. However, doctors have been able to resist governments' attempts to change the system in different ways. Harrison et al (1992) refer to the 'macropower' of doctors operating through national pressure groups such as the BMA and the Royal Colleges who bargain with the state, and the 'micropower' of doctors who operate at individual and local levels as the 'gatekeepers' to the health care system. The mythologising of medicine - the belief in doctors as Gods, the kudos given to medical elites and the reinforcement of medical power through socialisation (Zola 1972, Illich 1976) all mean that doctors are often able to avoid having to use the first face of power.

There is a danger however in overstating the extent to which the socialisation of medicine allows medical elites to exercise power in less visible ways. The role of uncertainty in the health care system and the way it interacts with the forces of power makes an important contribution to the understanding of policy and decision making. There is considerable uncertainty within the health care system concerning health needs, health status and the appropriateness of alternative therapies (Mooney and Loft 1989). Lipsky (1980) argues that where there are high levels of uncertainty then variations in responses are found to be more acceptable and the influence of centralised power is lessened. This has important implications for interpretations of the NHS that see it moving from a Fordist to a post-Fordist culture where direct centralised control is replaced by more fragmented structures (Harrison et al 1992). The relationship between uncertainty, power and shifts in culture within the NHS is reflected in the 'macropower' of doctors coming into open conflict with the government through the BMA whilst the micro-power of doctors is still able to operate to resist change. Gaining insights into the ways in which power, uncertainty and culture interact provides opportunities for interpreting policy processes.

The 'hidden' nature of some of these relationships make Habermas' critical project highly relevant to policy analysis.

Habermas and communicative ethics

The relevance of the Habermasian project to the analysis of health policy is found in the insights it can give into the distortions of communication by powerful groups, (the colonisation of the lifeworld by medicine being an example), and the opportunities for health care policy that would arise as a consequence of achieving undistorted communication (Scambler 1987). For Habermas, linguistic communication between individuals contains implicit 'validity claims' in that what is said is comprehensible, spoken with sincerity, its propositional content is true and it is justified. The first two of these can be defended by individual behaviour whilst the last two can be defended in dialogue; they are 'discursively redeemable'. When all four of these validity claims are met then undistorted communication is being entered into, what Habermas calls the 'ideal speech' situation (Habermas 1979). Habermas places reliance on truth being achieved through consensus in an ideal speech situation (White 1988).[1]

It should be clear that this is a procedural theory and that "practical discourse is a procedure for testing the validity of hypothetical norms, not for producing justified norms" (Habermas 1990 p122). For Habermas the validity of a statement can be justified by means of a three stage analysis through claims to truth (concerning the objective world), claims of rightness (concerning the shared world) and claims of truthfulness (concerning the subjective world). Critics of Habermas see this as idealistic in that it is unable to grasp the extent to which power discourses invade all speech situations, (Lukes 1982, Keat 1981). Habermas' response to this is that his position reflects a goal and not an actual state of affairs and that his theory can form the basis of a critical analysis of communicative practices. The aim is the exposure of systematic distortions so that the exercise of power and dominance can be revealed as 'ideology' or 'false consciousness'. However, the practical effect of setting up an idealised situation is to separate power relations from communicative relations. The danger is that power is then seen as being located in words and not in the institutional context in which they are used (Bourdieu 1991). This highlights the dangers of adopting an uncritical view of Habermas' idealisation.

Habermas makes a distinction between two forms of rational action, 'purposive rational' action and 'communicative' action. The former represents a technical rationality analogous to Weber's *Zweckrationalitat* and is embedded in social systems such as welfare systems, and markets. Communicative action is a form of linguistic interaction aimed at achieving understanding. The paradox of rationality for Habermas is that social systems colonise the 'life-world' (where social interaction and culture are sustained and reproduced) with rationality that has positive and negative characteristics and effects (Thompson 1984). This can be seen in the way medical expertise has colonised the life-world. This has occurred through the social respect attributed to medical expertise which itself is legitimised and founded upon a form of formal knowledge which presents itself as 'purposive rational' action (Friedson 1986). The positive aspects of this rationality are to be found in the contribution it makes to meeting generalisable interests whilst the negative aspects can be found in the inappropriate use of formal medical knowledge to justify or legitimate the vested interests of the powerful. In this sense ' formal knowledge' becomes 'ideology'.

Now the distinctions I have made here are not as clear and precise as I have so far implied. Certainly the work of Foucault should cause us to pause at this point to consider whether it is possible to distinguish between different types of rationality when the effects of power may be all pervasive (Rabinow 1984). In his analysis of power Foucault searched for those who resist established practices of power to gain the perspective of a counterpower. He was careful however to state that every counterpower moves with the horizon of the power it challenges and at the point of transformation into a new power complex it also stimulates a new counterpower. In this way Foucault resisted the temptation to take sides and was dismissive of those who interpret power as evil or bad and those upon which power is exercised as good (Levy 1977). For Foucault, power was productive. It is not necessarily a repressive force but creative in the sense that it is the means whereby knowledge, forms of pleasure and discourse, happen. Power is a force that:

> is exercised only over free subjects, and only in so far as they
> are free. (Foucault 1982, p. 220)

In this sense his interpretation of power seems to contain constraining aspects, but in its relationship to knowledge, power by virtue of "multiple forms of constraint" is an inherent part of the production of truth (Foucault 1980). This allows Foucault to argue that medical practitioners (to take one example) have been able to classify, observe and experiment on the bodies of subjects (be they patients or populations) by means of a set of power relations that provide the means to further knowledge and at the same time take that knowledge into judicial spheres to legitimise their claim to expand their areas of practice. It is here that we find an intermingling of claims to power and claims to knowledge (Philip 1985). Thus, through a multiplicity of such power relations, operating through institutions and human sciences (asylums and medicine being prime examples) power saturates the social field.

Foucault emphasised the way disciplinary power defines bodies subjecting them to normalisation through what he termed 'biopower'. This is an important point, for Foucault argued that biopower can function without having to resort to a false consciousness which could be tamed by critical discourse. If we accept this analysis then anyone working in Marxist and Freudian traditions using distinctions such as legitimate and illegitimate and conscious and unconscious motives, to fight the 'dark forces' of repression are themselves in danger of reinforcing the violent effects of normalisation on the body. If this is so, then why and how should we engage in political opposition? Foucault started to develop criteria for addressing this problem based on anti disciplinarian rights that are free from the constraints of sovereignty (Foucault 1980). But Foucault's critique of modern power could only be constructed by reference to normative notions and it is difficult to see how he could escape this (Fraser 1981). It is this that leads Habermas to argue that the development of normative structures in connection with the modern formation of power were ignored by Foucault (Habermas 1992). Giddens argues that in focusing on power, discipline and surveillance Foucault leaves little room for the concept of agency or the individual embodying it (Giddens 1982). He goes on to argue that institutions such as hospitals did not appear as if from nowhere "behind the backs" of those agents who built them. This is contested however, for Foucault was concerned with processes of self-formation in which persons were active (Foucault 1982, Rabinow 1984). In light of these points, if we are to utilise critical theory to gain insights into how power operates in the NHS it is necessary to recognised that the distinctions I have outlined earlier are clouded by the operation of power within the system.

Communicative ethics and power

Habermas' project sees critical theory working towards exposing the operation of the hidden faces of power. This is an ambitious project fraught with complexities but Habermas seems to suggest that the analysis of speech acts has potential to form a basis for the analysis of power. In his analysis Habermas makes a distinction between communicative action and strategic action (Habermas 1984). Communicative action is a form of linguistic interaction where all the communicants perform actions in speech with the aim of achieving consensus and understanding. It is only in communicative action that all speech acts contain validity claims concerning comprehensibility, sincerity, truth and justification, which are openly criticizable and discursively redeemable. Strategic action on the other hand, occurs when at least one of the communicants aims to produce an effect on the others through speech acts. The aim of strategic action is therefore success. Open strategic action occurs where the speakers intention to influence and have an effect on the listener(s) is openly declared. Concealed strategic action occurs where there is no such open declaration and involves deception. This can be conscious deception whereupon the speaker manipulates the speech act to give the impression of communicative action whilst pursuing the goal of successfully influencing the listener(s). It can also take the form of unconscious deception where the speaker engages in self-deception concerning the aims of his speech act. How such forms of deception can be assessed in practice is, of course, a major problem. More important perhaps is the danger of assuming a privileged position for assessing speech acts (not only the speech acts of others but one's own speech acts). Such an objective position is impossible in practice and untenable in theory.

Habermas' analysis presents us with a formal guide for interrogating discourses of power. Scambler (1987) explores the relevance of Habermas' theory to the medicalization of the life-world in the experience of pregnancy and childbirth. He relates Habermas' concern with new social movements to the success of women's and users' groups in challenging medical interests in the field of obstetrics and gynaecology. He counsels caution however, stating that the capacity of the medical establishment to absorb changes whilst retaining their power should not be underestimated. It is through the increasing power and influence of the medical industrial complex that the relationship between the colonisation and rationalisation of the life world is cemented. The Habermasian project gives a strong emphasis on the need to empower social movements and has parallels with 'bottom up' approaches to health policy and health needs.

The basis for discussing health care needs

If there is agreement over giving priority to need satisfaction as a goal then policy makers must face the problem of how to agree on the best strategy for achieving this goal. A number of questions immediately arise from this. In the first instance there is a need to know how effective particular technologies are in achieving goals. The issue of who should control their development and use is pertinent to a policy framework that has participation at its roots. Policy makers need to know what are the appropriate social policies to satisfy needs e.g. prevention versus cure. As a back drop to this of course is the problem of whether it is possible to meet needs within a resource constraint. These questions are confounded by lobbying, conflicts of interest and conflicts between individual, moral and professional interests.

Within Doyal and Gough's theory of needs, communicative action is seen as a prerequisite to decision making that involves conflicts over needs (Doyal and Gough 1991). Decisions should emerge from debates that yield the most rational and efficient solution to the problem of needs satisfaction in any particular context. Such debates must occur in an open and critical communicative process involving disagreement in a way that demonstrates objective acceptability of some forms of consensus.

The focus on autonomy and equality in a needs based policy framework demands a commitment to political democracy. There are clear conflicts here, the tyranny of the majority over the minority being one. Another is the threat of a strong centralised planning structure to individual autonomy. On the other hand a completely decentralised democracy could place limits on the kind of long-term planning efficiency which needs satisfaction demands. Decentralised decision making may also lead to variations in levels of provision resulting in geographical inequity. To tackle these problems as part of a theory of need, Habermas' ideal speech situations could be used in an attempt to focus on a means of enhancing the rationality of needs based policy debates. For Habermas the problem of reason is identifying the principles by which the most effective policies for meeting 'generalisable interests' can be determined. In light of this Doyal and Gough proposed three rules for rational and democratic discussion of needs:

1   All participants should possess the best available understanding concerning the technical issues raised by whatever problem they're trying to solve"

2   If disputes about such knowledge threaten the optimisation of need satisfaction, their rational resolution will require specific methodological and communicational skills" [controlled trials (methodological) - hermeneutic understanding, practical understanding and pragmatic rules of truth telling (communicational)].

3   Communication intended to lead to improved technical and practical understanding - and thus the possibility of optimising need satisfaction - must be as democratic as possible. (see page 122 A Theory of Human Need).

Doyal and Gough's rules are an attempt to operationalise Habermas' communicative ethics. In doing this they can be criticised for adopting a naive view of the struggles over needs in late capitalist societies. What form should the 'democratic communication' that Doyal and Gough envisage take? Can we rely on 'pragmatic rules of truth telling' to address the forces of institutional power, when those forces are producing the "rhetoric of expert needs discourses" (Fraser 1981 p174). These questions highlight the problems and pitfalls of attempts to base policy on ideal states. Schlosberg (1995) uses the example of the Community Board Program of San Francisco to argue that communicative practices can be seen as "an expression of and an ongoing guide for emancipatory struggle and practices" (p311). However, he also identifies a tension between the recognition of diversity and difference by such emancipatory groups and Habermas' emphasis on universalization and ultimate consensus. Despite this, Habermas' work can still provide us with a basis for evaluating communicative practices. In this respect Doyal and Gough's rules do represent a useful starting point for examining the ways in which needs are discussed in practice. It is to a practical example of the discussion of needs that we turn to in the next chapter.

Note

1   The ideal speech situation is formally operationalised as claims of truth telling by the following rules:

1. Each subject who is capable of speech and action is allowed to participate in discourses.

2. a) Each is allowed to call into question any proposal.
   b) Each is allowed to introduce any proposal into the discourse
   c) Each is allowed to express her attitudes, wishes and needs.

3. No speaker ought to be hindered by compulsion - whether arising from inside or outside of it - from making use of the rights secure under 1 and 2.

From these rules Habermas proceeds to assert that:

A. Whoever engages in argumentation presupposes the validity of the discourse act
B. When argumentation concerns norms, actors must admit (or otherwise contradict themselves) that universalization is the only rule under which norms will be taken by each to be legitimate.

4 Assessing need and planning health services: the case of renal services

Introduction

Following the publication of *The Tomlinson Report* (Tomlinson 1992) the London Implementation Group[1] established six specialty review groups to examine the provision of key tertiary services in Greater London. As one of these six specialty reviews, renal services were clearly identified as an area where rationalisation of services needed careful planning. The renal specialty review was set up in March 1993 and reported in June 1993. The aim of the review group was to assess current and projected needs for the specialty, to develop criteria for the development of major tertiary centres and to advise on the future pattern of service provision including the location of major centres in order to achieve the most effective services for the local resident population (Renal Review Group, *Report of the Review of the London Renal Services 1993*).[2] The review group perceived its main purpose to determine whether services to patients with kidney disease in London were appropriate.[3] This chapter sets the scene by taking a critical look at the way in which the group defined the health care needs of the existing and potential renal patient population and the criteria it used to inform its decision making. In doing this the model for future service provision recommended by the group is situated within a historical, economic and geo-political context in order to discuss its main motivating factors. Most importantly the group's technical knowledge of needs is related to the framework for operationalising needs used by Doyal and Gough. The review group was only able to work with the data available to it at the time. Knowledge of the epidemiology and aetiology of renal disease is continually evolving; this discussion does not take account of developments occurring in the years following the review.

Membership of the group

The chairman of the group was a Professor of Renal medicine with an international reputation, highly respected by his peers, who had been involved in epidemiological studies of need for renal services and modelling renal services. The other clinicians on the group all had specialist knowledge of renal services as well as membership and influence within professional bodies that brought skills to the group and legitimacy in terms of 'peer respect'. The managers on the group comprised a chief executive of a recently merged purchasing authority and a Department of Health civil servant who had played a considerable part in drafting the Tomlinson report. This invested a managerial legitimacy in the group as well as providing it with access to a 'network' of managerial and physician links across London, and beyond, that were clearly used by the group at different times to 'smooth the waters', promote co-operation and minimise conflict. The nurse manager on the group was experienced in reviewing nursing services and again brought legitimacy to the review of nursing services. The group also had a 'patient representative' as a member: a Director of the National Kidney Research Fund. During its deliberations the group sought support from other clinicians, management consultants, epidemiologists and health service researchers. In drawing these people together the chairman was concerned to ensure 'technical' legitimacy for the group by the membership having the respect of peers and by the final decision being informed by the best knowledge base available, given the time constraints they were working under. There also appeared to be a concern to ensure that the group had individual members who were capable of challenging orthodoxy and more importantly to be seen by others as representing challenging interests. The dynamics of the group will be discussed further in the next chapter.

Main recommendations of the renal review group's report

One of the main concerns that informed the review group's recommendations was the current provision and future need for renal services. The group's analysis of epidemiology, geography and access to services led to the view that the present siting of renal services in the capital created inequity of access. Services had to be moved out of the teaching hospitals to areas that were closer to patient populations. This had to be balanced however, with the group's concern to preserve and develop teaching and transplantation services both of which, it was felt, needed a critical mass of service provision. The solution to preserving this balance was called the 'hub and spoke' model of service provision. This envisaged

61

specialist University transplant centres at the core in inner London (hub) and satellite units doing basic dialysis located outwards closer to populations (the spokes) but with support from the specialist mother units. The London area was split into five crude geographic sectors, South-East, North-East, North-Central, West and South-West with a central core of five tertiary referral centres (one in each sector). The sectors followed the boundaries of the existing Thames Regions with the North Central sector dissecting the boundary between the two North Thames Regions. This fitted with the teaching hospital groupings recommended in the Tomlinson report. Each centre would provide a transplant service for approximately 3 million people, expert nephrology for some 1.5 million people and provide Renal Replacement Therapy (RRT) support for at least 80 new patients per annum. Five autonomous centres were also thought to be required, sited strategically and predominantly in the shire counties. These would provide the same services as the central core but without transplant or academic provision. It was thought that one such unit per 3 million population was required. The proposed network of 'satellite' units would link each to either a teaching centre or an autonomous centre. The group considered the staffing and facilities available at each unit in detail and recommended that in the five core units the staffing structure and bed complement be in place within a specific time scale ranging from one to three years according to each unit. The siting of the core units was specified in the report. Suggestions for the siting of autonomous centres were mentioned but it was accepted that the decision on these would ultimately rest with purchasers and providers.

Siting of teaching/transplant core units

The decision on the siting of core units was based on a number of criteria. The consideration of a site's potential for future multi-disciplinary work and future academic excellence was given a high priority. The group was not able to make a decision on the basis of comparative costs of service provision in different units due to the generally poor quality of costing data provided by units. Sites were selected with the aim of sustaining and creating opportunities for clinical service and research. At a basic level therefore, equity of access considerations, tempered by the need to maintain critical mass, determined the development of a model for renal service provision in the capital. However, once the model was decided upon, the siting of units was largely justified by reference to standards of clinical service and research.

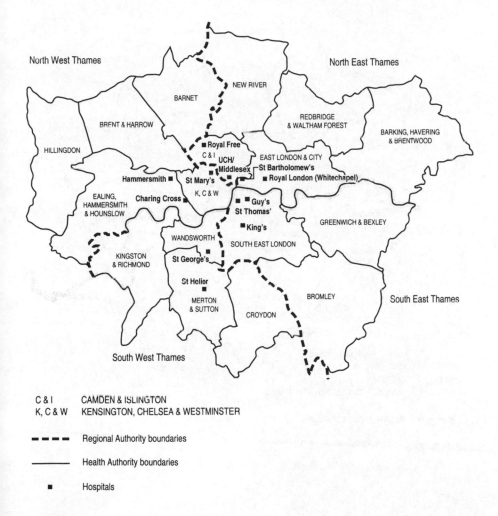

Figure 4.1 Main specialty centres: service configuration at time of review. Source: *Renal Review* 1993 (Jones 1995b).

North West Thames

North East Thames

NEW RIVER

BARNET

BRENT & HARROW

HILLINGDON

C & I

UCH/
Middlesex

REDBRIDGE
& WALTHAM FOREST

BARKING, HAVERING
& BRENTWOOD

EAST LONDON & CITY

Hammersmith ■

■ Royal London (Whitechapel)

EALING,
HAMMERSMITH
& HOUNSLOW

K, C & W

Charing Cross ■

■ Guy's
St Thomas'

GREENWICH & BEXLEY

WANDSWORTH

SOUTH EAST LONDON

KINGSTON
& RICHMOND

St George's ■

BROMLEY

South East Thames

MERTON
& SUTTON

CROYDON

South West Thames

C & I   CAMDEN & ISLINGTON
K, C & W   KENSINGTON, CHELSEA & WESTMINSTER

▬ ▬ ▬ ▬   Regional Authority boundaries

─────────   Health Authority boundaries

■   Hospitals

Figure 4.2 Main specialty centres: proposed service configuration.
Source: *Renal Review* 1993 (Jones 1995b).

Figures 4.1 and 4.2 show the configuration of services in London before and after the recommendations of the review group. In the South-East sector Guy's/St Thomas' trust was recommended, in the North-East the Royal London Hospital (RLH) was preferred as a site for a merged St Bartholomew's and RLH unit. In the North-Central sector the preferred site was University College Hospital/Middlesex, whilst in the South-West the chosen site was St George's. Finally in the Western sector the Hammersmith Hospital, with a link to a nephrology service at Charing Cross, was favoured. Services at King's, Royal Free, St Bartholomew's, St Mary's and St Helier's either faced closure, a reduction in size or merger with other units. The rationalisation of services was presented not as a cut in services but as a re-provision eventually leading to an expansion in patient numbers.

General recommendations

The group also made general recommendations covering staffing, teaching, prevention and the quality of care. The review was critical of the quality of nursing in the capital's renal units and made a number of specific recommendations for future staffing structures. The final group report suggested that in terms of monitoring quality, purchasing authorities should require prospective audit of quality of treatment using survival curve analysis as well as more detailed analysis of the efficiency of dialysis techniques. The group also recommended the setting up of a national registry of renal patients.

In terms of purchasing renal services the group recommended that because of the low volume and high cost nature of renal treatment, health authorities should consider forming consortia to purchase services. This, it was felt, would allow a more stable market to operate. The purchasing authorities would contract with tertiary or district nephrology centres who would then have the responsibility for making arrangements with satellite units. This reflected the ongoing debate that group members had about how the recommendations made in the report could come to fruition in a quasi-market system.

Definition of 'need'

The main body of work used to inform the renal group's decision making focused on the population need for renal replacement therapy (RRT). The epidemiological approach to needs assessment was therefore given a high priority in the groups deliberations. The review used a 'gold standard' of population need for RRT, based on the Renal Association's recommendations (Renal Association 1991), of 80 new cases per million population per year under age 80. The Renal Association's recommended rate was itself derived from studies that had identified unmet need for services in Devon, Lancashire and Northern Ireland (Feest et al 1990, McGeown 1990). The group concluded that the overall population need in the Thames Regions was likely to be greater than the national estimate of 80 per million because of the ethnic composition of the population, and considered 90-100 million to be a more realistic figure.

The Feest data (based on populations in Blackburn, Exeter and North Devon) and the McGeown data (based on the population of Northern Ireland) came from areas where the proportion of minority ethnic groups in the population was low or where the average age of people from minority ethnic groups was low. The group stressed that it was essential to consider the variation between districts in population need and their access to current treatment when deciding on the future location of renal services. Age and ethnicity were considered the important socio-demographic factors determining population need for RRT and these were reviewed in detail in the report. The effect of socio-economic factors was not considered by the group because no information was available on the socio-economic characteristics of renal patients in the Thames Regions and there was very little literature on this aspect of renal disease. Knowledge of the relationship between social class and renal failure was limited although a weak association was found between lower social class and chronic renal failure in one Scottish study (McCormick and Navarro 1973).

In the survey by Feest et al (1990) the incidence of advanced chronic renal failure was estimated using a blood serum creatinine level of greater than 500mmol/l as an indicator. In people aged less than 80 it was estimated that 78 new patients per million would need dialysis annually. The study also demonstrated a marked increase in incidence of chronic renal failure with age. The survey by McGeown used a questionnaire to General Practitioners to identify the need for treatment. Both studies derived estimates of the population in need for renal replacement therapy based on those patients considered suitable for treatment whether they received it or not.

The Feest figure of 78 new patients per million was arrived at once those considered not suitable for treatment were removed. The proportion of those not considered suitable increased with age (51% of patients aged 60-80 years were not referred). These figures were similar to the estimates made by McGeown.

In the Feest study the authors estimated that 29 (54%) out of 54 patients not referred under the age of 80 should have been referred for treatment. It is important to note that the elderly are a group where thresholds for treatment change. The incidence of disease in the elderly (in excess of 200 per million population per year) is far in excess of the numbers of elderly accepted for Renal Replacement Therapy (RRT). In the UK in 1991, only 60.7 new patients per million were being treated (Renal Association 1991). This suggested 'unmet need' amounting to at least 20 new patients per million population per year. In addition, the work done by both Feest and McGeown suggested that these are mostly high risk or elderly patients. It was in light of these figures that the Renal Association recommended a target rate of 80 patients per million under age 80 and this figure was used as a baseline for the renal review group's comparative work.

Critical analysis of the definition of need

The definition of population need used by the review group raises two major questions. Firstly the level of need used was defined by reference to the most recent and most relevant epidemiological studies which had received recognition and acceptance by the medical profession. The legitimacy of the figures produced by these studies was confirmed by the figure of 80 new patients per million being adopted by the Renal Association as a target. There was therefore an apparent medical consensus on what the level of population need should be and the legitimacy of this consensus was validated by reference to the epidemiological studies that supported it. Secondly, the studies considered whether patients were suitable or not for treatment. Decisions about suitability were made by the physicians involved in the research on the basis of their reviewing patient notes. The need for care was therefore determined by a medically defined cut-off based on whether treatment was considered beneficial or not. Clinical benefit as perceived by physicians was therefore an important determining factor in defining levels of need. There may however be variation in the 'thresholds' for referring patients to renal services as defined by general practitioners, general physicians and renal physicians. The studies did not give clear details of how thresholds for treatment were agreed upon. Given the capacity for disagreement among physicians about whom to treat and not to treat (Parsons and Lock 1980), the medically defined 'cut-off' should not be construed as definitive. Comparisons with other countries also show that higher rates are achievable (Baker 1993). This was acknowledged by group members. Nevertheless, in terms of medical consensus (containing some provisos) on 'need' at a point in time, the figure of 80 per million had considerable weight. It is significant that at no point during the group's deliberations was this figure questioned by the managers in the group. If we consider that the estimates of the number of people who could benefit from RRT during the 1970s and early 1980s were 40 new patient per million population per annum (Branch et al 1971, Halper 1989) then the definition of need used by the review group may be more transient and susceptible to revision than was originally thought. The group's own epidemiological analysis adds weight to this view.

Demographic and epidemiological analysis

The main demographic factors associated with ESRF are age and ethnicity. Incidence is estimated to be high in areas with high proportions of the elderly and ethnic minorities. Afro-Caribbeans, Bangladeshis and Far East Asian groups all have risk factors such as hypertension, Systemic Lupus Erythematosis (SLE) and Non Insulin Dependent Diabetes (NIDDM) which make them particularly vulnerable to renal disease (Melia et al 1991). To examine the demographic profile of patients currently receiving RRT in the Thames Regions the group asked each renal unit in the Regions and those bordering the Regions to supply a profile of new patients accepted on to their programmes for the calendar years 1991 and 1992 and of all patients receiving renal replacement therapy on the unit's programme at the end of 1992/early 1993. Acceptances are the number of patients taken on to RRT in any one year and can then be presented as a rate for a population. The number of patients alive and on RRT at a point in time can also be presented as a rate. The demographic profile produced by the group was based on the patient's District Health Authority of residence, age, ethnicity and diabetic status. This allowed a geographical and epidemiological analysis of renal disease to be drawn together looking at risk factors, associated disease, demography and access to services.

The acceptance and prevalence rates for districts in the Thames Regions showed an overall acceptance rate of 74 per million. This showed marked geographic variation, from 51 per million in the Shires, 82 per million in Outer London and 110 per million in Inner London. Acceptance rates significantly higher than the target rate of 80 per million were found in the Districts of Harrow, Parkside, West Lambeth, Camberwell, Lewisham and North Southwark whilst rates significantly below 60 per million were found in the Shire Districts of North Bedfordshire, North East Essex, Mid Essex and Maidstone. Inaccuracies in the data (both unit and census data), closer proximity of 'Blacks' and 'Asians' to units and increased rates of disease in 'Blacks' and 'Asians' were all considered as factors explaining the differences in rates. There was some discussion in the group as to the extent to which the proximity of 'Blacks' and 'Asians' to renal units affected referral rates. There was a significant correlation between acceptance rates of Greater London districts and their respective proportions of all ethnic minorities but the group's timescale and data limitations meant that it was not possible to estimate the proportion of geographic variation accounted for by age and ethnicity. This evidence, coupled with concern among group members about poor accessibility to health services among ethnic groups led to the view that higher rates of disease was the most likely explanatory factor.

Access

Distance of residence from renal services has a significant effect on rates of service use. Indeed a study of service use in NETRHA found a correlation between the average acceptance rates and travelling distance to the nearest unit (NETRHA 1990). This study was unable to control for the composition of populations. Other studies had confirmed that uptake was lower in districts without a renal centre compared with districts with renal centres (Feest et al 1990) and found a correlation between acceptance rates for new patients and distance to unit (Dalziel and Garret 1987). The mapping of prevalence and acceptance rates by DHA allowed a limited analysis of equity of access to services to be made. The review group placed considerable emphasis on travel times to units, seeing this as a marker for evaluating access. The review found wide variations in patient travelling times and distances with some patients taking 1 hour to travel 4 miles and others travelling 85 miles in 2.5 hours. Using average distances and times of patients using hospital car services, a hidden cost of £613,043 was estimated.

After much debate amongst group members, travel costs to patients were not seen as NHS costs and were not included in service costings, but travel times were perceived as a cost on the quality of patient life. This was used to back up arguments for services to be sited closer to patients in satellite units. The group recommended however, that the choice of the most appropriate sites for sub-regional District General Hospitals and satellite units be made at a local level. This reflected its concerns to get consensus on a model for renal provision and on the selection of five teaching centres in London, rather than being prescriptive about which other sites in the Thames regions should be chosen for expansion.

Modelling

The prevalence of patients on RRT in the UK was 331 per million population at the end of 1990. A 'steady state' situation for RRT would exist when the number entering and leaving the process equalise. A study by Bolger and Davies (1992) had presented a model of demand and supply for renal services and estimated that under existing conditions the prevalence of patients would increase by 40% before the turn of the century. It should be noted however, that thresholds varied between units and this model applied to one specific area. In addition the model and the information used within it had been criticised for being inaccurate, (Feest and Harrison 1992). A model for planning growth in the prevalence of patients was designed for the review group using techniques developed by Wood et al (1980 and 1987). This was used in preference to Bolger's simulation models which were believed to provide less opportunity for understanding by non-specialist planners. The Wood model used a threefold definition of renal patients:

Low Risk	-	under 55 non-diabetic
Medium Risk	-	55-64 non diabetic or diabetic under 55
High Risk	-	65 and over or diabetic 55 and over

Low and medium risk patients were considered suitable for transplantation but high risk patients were not. Risks were defined in terms of patient survival and probability of transplant failure. The model was refined following discussion by renal group members and used to provide five-year estimates for growth from current prevalence levels. This was used to reinforce the perception of likely increases in demand on services in the future. The eventual steady state position with an acceptance rate of 80 per million was modelled at 11,638 patients with 7,417 on dialysis. With an acceptance rate of 100 per million however, the model predicted a steady state of 13,304 patients with 9,083 on dialysis. This contrasted with the existing Thames patient population of 5,778 with 2,700 on dialysis. The review therefore relied on a medical definition of need and applied a 'risk' analysis to this definition using techniques that had been tried and tested in the past. This risk analysis was then used to predict future demand for services, thus ensuring a strong link between medically defined need and predicted demand within a 'rational' framework. The argument presented by the group, on the basis of this, amounted to 'unmet need' existing at present and that an expansion in resources was required, but that the eventual steady state position would ensure that problems of 'infinite demands' would be manageable.

Transplantation

Transplantation was considered to be the most cost-effective treatment option for ESRF (West 1991) offering the opportunity for a better quality of life for most renal patients. In terms of patient needs and equity of provision therefore the availability and quality of transplantation services was an important issue for the review group. Thirteen NHS units in the Thames Regions were transplanting kidneys into adults at the time of the renal review. The review group examined their workload, staffing and survival data. Transplant activity in the Thames Regions was considered to be relatively high totalling 485 transplants per annum. There were wide variations between units in the size of activity, the proportion of patients transplanted who were elderly and the proportion of transplant patients from ethnic groups. The issue of ethnic differences in transplantation was not considered in detail by the group although there were clear concerns about the fairness of transplantation policies (Purviance 1993). Outcome data also varied with patient survival ranging from 79% to 96% and graft survival from 73% to 94% after the first year. The group judged that, allowing for case-mix, these figures were not below average and some units had exceptionally good crude rates. The group was however, struck by the high levels of resources required to maintain this activity particularly with respect to nurse staffing.

Any expansion of transplants is dependent on the pool of available donors. The number of patients waiting in the UK for a kidney transplant at December 1992 was 4,364 (Poulter 1993, source UKTSSA). There was already a perceived national need to increase the availability of organs and a number of recommendations had been made at a national level to increase the 'harvest rate' (Gore et al 1989). Since April 1992 the NHS management executive reimbursed units maintaining donors to cover the extra costs involved in obtaining donor kidneys but a number of factors act against increasing donor numbers. The group thought it unlikely that cadaver organ availability would exceed 40 per million population in the foreseeable future, and at that rate the population of the Thames Regions would yield an expected 600 transplants per annum. The group took advice from the Royal Colleges of Surgeons and Physicians and the British Transplantation Society, and concluded that each transplant centre should conduct at least 100 donor grafts per year. This represented the sense of a 'critical mass' necessary to ensure high quality transplantation services. Some units raised the concern that the group's proposals would lead to very large units with large numbers of patients. The group's report stressed that this was not what was envisaged, and that the core units should only provide tertiary, specialist and transplant care. Under this scenario, the number of patients treated in central London would decrease as more geographically accessible units became available, and consultants developed outreach clinics closer to the patient populations.

Academic appraisal

The group considered the academic excellence of the London units in some detail. Details on the funding and research activities of each unit were scrutinised and advice was taken from funding bodies, and from national and international authorities in academic renal medicine. The relative research ratings of general medical departments were also noted. The academic appraisal had a considerable influence over the decision of where to site the five central core units. The group came to a consensus on the Royal Postgraduate Medical School and University College Hospital having the strongest academic base. The strength of the academic reputation of St

71

Thomas' and Guy's was given considerable weighting in the group's decision and there was a strong academic argument for relocating the large unit at St Helier to St George's. The reasoning behind this academic exercise was to protect and develop the academic and research base of London. The group was at pains to undertake the academic review in as objective way as possible and to ensure that the London units saw it as a fair and objective exercise. As we shall see in the review of the group's meetings however, the weighting given to the academic exercise for some units came into conflict with the review's opinion of those units in other areas of evaluation.

Costs

The review group requested business plans from each unit in the Thames Regions for 1992/93 and 1993/94 and details of service costings. The aim was to compare the cost-effectiveness of the different units and come to some conclusion on comparative costs. Unfortunately the group received a poor response from all but two of the units. Review group members had more accurate information from units outside the Thames Regions and it was decided that a pragmatic alternative would be to construct 'built cost' profiles from these other centres and apply those as a costing template for the services proposed in London.

Consultation with Patient Groups

The review invited views and comments from the National Federation of Kidney Patients Associations (NFKPA), British Kidney Patient Association (BKPA) and the twelve London based Kidney Patients Associations (KPAs), of whom ten replied. The general response was summarised in the review group report showing support for dialysis in the patient's home and for satellite units. The level of services contained in tertiary centres, including staffing levels, was stipulated in detail. The responses stressed the need for accessibility, timeliness and communication placing emphasis on the need to 'continually improve patient information, knowledge and awareness regarding treatment'. Finally the role of social workers and the need to assess employment opportunities for renal patients was stressed. The review group's report only listed the 12 renal patient associations consulted. Their responses were not reproduced in detail. Whilst supporting the principle of getting services closer to patients the KPA responses often concentrated on supporting the case for their particular unit to be retained. This raised a number of questions concerning the consultation exercise. It clearly did not represent an adequate consultation and the KPA responses were not discussed in detail during the review groups deliberations although the Chairman was at pains to retain dialogue with patient representatives at all times. The limitations of the exercise will be discussed in the next chapter.

Critical analysis of the review

This section places the renal review group's work in a historical, economic and geo-political context comparing UK health care policy with respect to renal services with those in other Western countries. In this way the main exogenous pressures on the group influencing their decisions will be highlighted. The 'rational' basis for constructing a future model for services that fitted with the imperatives of a quasi-market will be critically assessed.

The history of ESRF treatment in UK had been one of under referral and under supply compared with other countries (Wing et al 1982, Wing 1983, Halper 1989). This led to the criticism that the British health care system used age based rationing to deny care to those most likely to need RRT and that access to treatment was arbitrary and inequitable (Baker 1993). UK policies changed considerably in the 1980s however, and since 1984 there was an increase in the proportion of new patients being treated annually. In 1991 the UK treated 3,430 new patients which was the third highest number of the countries registered with EDTA. However, acceptance rates at the time of the renal review show that the UK had a rate of 59.7 patients per million which ranked fifteenth; many countries having rates in excess of 75 new patients per million (see table 4.1).

It is also important to note that within the UK acceptance rates varied considerably between regions and acceptance rates were higher for men than for women. Again, comparisons were difficult because of differences in ethnic composition and social class. The majority of under referrals were in high risk categories (elderly and diabetics) but between 1980 and 1985 the proportion of patients in these 'high risk' groups increased considerably, although the UK still had lower rates than several European countries. In 1986 the acceptance rate per million population in the UK for patients aged 65-74 was 112 for men and 57 for women. This did not compare favourably with other European countries (see table 4.2).

Table 4.1
Summary of new patients accepted for
renal replacement therapy (RRT) during 1991 in Europe

Country	Number of new patients in 1991	Per million population
Israel	493	106.3
Austria	805	105.3
Sweden	852	99.6
Switzerland	639	95.5
Germany (West)	5771	94.1
Belgium	868	86.7
Portugal	887	85.5
Luxembourg	30	79.4
France	4350	77.1
Greece	709	70.6
Cyprus	47	67.0
Norway	47	67.0
Germany (East)	1045	62.6
Netherlands	896	60.0
United Kingdom	**3430**	**59.7**
Spain	2341	59.5
Czechoslovakia	873	55.7
Finland	271	54.4
Italy	3105	53.9
Iceland	13	50.4

Source: EDTA - quoted in Poulter 1993

Table 4.2
Acceptance rates per million population in patients aged 65-74 in 1986

Country	Men	Women
West Germany	225	153
Italy	208	117
Spain	160	98
France	132	90
UK	112	57

Source: Wing 1993

International differences in the mix of treatments offered by renal centres had been known for some time. Data from EDTA (1988) indicated a growth in services throughout Europe between 1971 and 1985 particularly in transplantation and CAPD. It had been argued previously that levels and methods of funding services were a major determinant of treatment policies (Simmons & Mrine 1984). In the UK the system of fixed budgets and smaller budgets per head of population had resulted in not only rationing of services in terms of number of patients treated but in a different mix of treatment options (Rennie et al 1985). The UK also had a lower number of renal centres per million population then other Western European Countries whilst the capacity for hospital haemodialysis within centres was lower in the UK.

As a result the UK dialysis programme differed considerably from those of other developed countries. As has been shown the situation during the 1970s was one of under provision. In the 1980s the UK expanded its dialysis programme considerably with the introduction of CAPD. This development was not reflected in the rest of Europe where expansion occurred through renal units as haemodialysis treatment centres. In the UK, the large number of patients on CAPD put different pressures on existing haemodialysis units where much work was directed towards preparing patients for CAPD and treating CAPD failures. This is what Greenwood et al (1992) termed the 'imbalance in the UK dialysis programme'. In the UK, hospital haemodialysis was less common accounting for 17% of patients in 1986 whereas for 11/33 countries in EDTA the figure was 70%. Transplantation was the most common treatment in the UK (50% of patients in 1986, the comparable figure for EDTA was 27%). For patients aged over 65 years, haemodialysis and CAPD were more common treatments in UK and for diabetics CAPD was more common. Table 4.3 compares the number of transplants carried out in a selection of European countries and shows the waiting list in those countries at 31st December 1992.

To address the imbalance in UK services there appeared to be a need for an expansion in haemodialysis facilities in decentralised units. Such a policy would inevitably place great strains on existing facilities particularly those based in teaching hospitals with large capital costs and overheads. An expansion in home haemodialysis seemed to be unlikely as the increase in demand would come from older and more vulnerable patients who needed more support than home haemodialysis could provide. Contracting out of dialysis had been pioneered in Wales. Such private ventures were considered a commercial success and were welcomed by the Renal Association. Nevertheless, there was a general awareness of the dangers in commercialisation of renal services linked to the drawbacks associated with monopoly suppliers and the restraints on clinical advancement.

Table 4.3
Kidney transplants in Europe 1991 and 1992

Country	Transplanted				Waiting List @ 31 December	
	1991	Rate pmp	1992	Rate pmp	1992	Rate pmp
Austria	389	51	306	40	1053	139
Belgium	378	38	330	33	901	90
Germany	2195	28	2034	26	7805	100
Luxembourg	7	19	3	8	23	61
Netherlands	426	29	428	29	1434	96
United Kingdom	1620	28	1622	28	4364	76

Source: Adapted from Poulter 1993, pmp=per million population.

Because of its over reliance on CAPD and the potential for expansion of unit haemodialysis the UK was seen as a unique market for private service providers. As pressure mounted to reallocate resources from large inner city teaching hospitals to purpose built centres, then competition to provide such services would clearly come not only from NHS providers but private hospitals and "large multinational companies like Baxter, Gambro and Fresenius" (Greenwood 1993). The NHS Management Executive on the other hand had suggested that the predicted expansion in patient numbers should be met through an expansion of CAPD. This view was criticised by Greenwood on the basis that the NHS figures were based on the characteristics of patients presently receiving RRT and 'perpetuated the myth' that CAPD was cheaper and was the treatment of choice for the elderly.

Clearly the predicted increase in demand for RRT, particularly among elderly and high risk patients, had considerable resource implications. To address the growth in patient numbers the review group had to balance demands for cost-containment from the management executive with the need to protect core services and the need to ensure that services appropriate to the needs of new patients were planned for. In Europe, survival rates for patients on all forms of RRT and all ages had increased since the 1970s. This was also true for the UK. Comparisons of survival rates between age groups were difficult, for those aged over 65 were likely to be selected differently and survival rates varied according to risk category. There were however large differences in survival rates between different countries though comparisons were made on the basis of crude rates. Opinions were divided on the effect of different levels of dialysis. In the USA the mortality rate among dialysis patients increased from 20.1% in 1983 to 24.3% in 1988 whilst average treatment length decreased over the same period. Greenwood (1993) suggested that USA providers operated an 'irresponsible' rationing policy as a result of a financial squeeze derived from the introduction of a prospective composite reimbursement system. He argued that failure to use urea kinetic modelling (UKM), as a method of monitoring a patient's dialysis needs, led to less dialysis being prescribed to malnourished patients. These patients needed more dialysis but their malnourishment was associated with low serum urea and creatinine thus on routine measurement they appeared to require less dialysis. Implicit in this was the fear that such practices could creep into the UK system; with the introduction of quasi-markets, the incentive was to accept as many patients as possible. Units were only able to maintain a certain prevalence of patients however and as the pressure to accept more patients increased there was potential pressure to 'compromise' dialysis policies:-

> Limiting access to haemodialysis, continuing patients on CAPD despite peritonitis, reduction of dialysis times and slippage from thrice into twice weekly dialysis schedules, without quality assurance by UKM, have all crept into UK practice over the last ten years...There are enough similarities with the USA to cause alarm. Clearly, forces are operating which can result in clinical compromise. (Greenwood et al 1992, p. 8)

UK policies may have had an adverse effect on survival rates. One study referred to the UK as having a 'go home for treatment or else die policy' (Rennie et al 1985) but clearly there had been marked improvements and changes in policy since. Outcome studies were limited however and needed to go beyond just survival to take into account quality of life including psycho-social implications and the effect of treatment on an individual's capacity to participate in their chosen form of life (Hardy et al 1991). Inter-treatment comparisons were in their infancy. Differences in the quality of life of patients on different modes of treatment were clearly difficult to interpret (Simmons et al 1988, Hart and Evans 1987) and subjective assessments of what patients valued most were considered likely to influence outcomes (Kutner et al 1986). Transplantation was considered to have the best survival rate, 80% at one year (Lancet 1990, editorial). The effect of market pressures on the quality of services and patient outcomes was a matter of concern for the review group. Data on patient survival was available but was not considered sensitive enough to be used in decision making. Similarly a policy decision was taken not to use outcome data, such as it was, to inform decision making. The main thrust of the groups thinking in this area seemed to be based on ensuring good outcomes through maintaining a 'high quality core service' in the central tertiary centres. Each renal unit was asked its view on this approach and there seemed to be a general acceptance that the difficulties of comparing outcomes for different case-mixes justified the exclusion of outcome data in the decision making process. The chair of the review group was meticulous in ensuring agreement on this. The apparent consensus however may have concealed some disputes for there was some variation in survival data and the performance of some units in relation to patient survival was considered sufficiently poor by some clinicians, based outside London, to be a basis for decision making.

Economic evaluation

Economic evaluations of renal treatment comparing survival data with cost per life year gained had been extensively reviewed, (West 1991, Ludbrook 1985, Mancini 1983). There was a feeling among some group members that economic evaluations were liable to become outdated very quickly. Ludbrook concluded that the method of financing services in the UK had resulted in more cost-effective patterns of care. Transplantation was considered to be the most cost-effective form of care, home dialysis and CAPD being the next most cost effective. However this was not taken as an argument to expand home dialysis and CAPD indiscriminately. Indeed the arguments about the under utilisation of hospital haemodialysis still remained as did the inappropriate allocation of patients with social problems or multi-system disease to home care. Estimates of the annual cost to the NHS of maintaining a patient on RRT are given in table 4.4.

Table 4.4
Cost estimates of treatments

Treatment modality	Annual Cost to NHS (1990 prices) £
Hospital Haemodialysis	18,000
Home Haemodialysis	11,000
CAPD	13,000
*Kidney transplant :	
Operation	10,000
Maintenance	3,000

* Operation is the cost in the first year of transplant, maintenance is the cost in every subsequent year
Source: West 1991

The use of lower cost treatments appeared to be more common in the UK than other Western European countries. However, it had also been argued that CAPD would appear less expensive because a large proportion of associated costs are incurred under other budgets e.g. GPs, Pharmacists, Social Services (Catalano et al 1990). Economic studies are difficult to undertake because patient selection is done rigorously and patients often switch between different modes of treatment. This not only complicates but often invalidates cost comparisons. Advances such as the use of cyclosporin as an immunosuppressive for post-transplant patients were often referred to by the clinicians on the group to highlight how technical advancements often run ahead of health service planning mechanisms. This reflected doubts and unease among the group concerning the permanency of the proposed model for services.

The review group received poor and inconsistent cost data from the units and it was decided that a cost comparison could not be undertaken. Nevertheless, the review was able to show that there was considerable under use of dialysis machines in London and that some units operated at very inefficient levels (*The Times* 1994). The only cost data used by the review group came from units outside the Thames regions. This was used to create an 'ideal' costing template for future services. This meant that the existing cost-effectiveness of units was not analysed as part of the group's evaluation. Given that there was a considerable body of work on the economics of RRT (Beech et al 1994) this represents a large gap in the group's knowledge base. There was some conflict between group members concerning the validity of past economic evaluations. In addition there was a feeling among some group members that the units were being deliberately obstructive in the limited financial data being made available to the review. After all the data was highly sensitive and, given the insecure position of many of the units in relation to the proposed rationalising of services in London, its publication had potentially disastrous consequences.

Implications of quasi-markets for renal services

The management of the finances of ESRF services had been reviewed prior to the implementation of the NHS reforms (Steele 1989, Mays 1990) but these reports could not deal with the likely effect of the new contracting systems on demand and supply for services. The reforms could have meant more competition with the private sector but private provision had not been found to be more effective or efficient although it had been found to be able to increase capacity more quickly in response to demand (Smith et al 1989). The opportunities for expansion that a market might bring were highlighted by Wing (1990). The tensions that these 'opportunities' created for a review group that was essentially engaged in a traditional 'Stalinist' planning exercise were considerable and will be discussed in the next chapter. It is clear that renal services in the UK had developed differently to those of other countries. The bureaucracy and overcentralisation of the UK system had been identified as a core factor in determining the pattern of provision (Baker 1993). Marked inequity in provision and poor access to services had also been a strong part of the UK picture and led to calls for provision of services to be closer to patients. The push to create a quasi-market created considerable uncertainty as responsibility for purchasing renal services was being devolved downwards from Regions to Districts. At one level it could be argued that this placed decision making at a closer level to patients and set up a market where decisions could be made explicitly. At another level it is possible that for large specialties such as renal medicine, devolving of decision making created greater bureaucracy and hindered the ability of decision makers to take a 'wider view'.

Evaluating the assessment of needs

The discussion so far has shown that the renal review group was planning future services in London in the context of considerable historical, geographical, economic and social forces. In the face of this the group was able to pull together a considerable amount of technical information on 'needs' for services. Need was defined in terms of incidence of disease, epidemiological risk and geographic access. Information on health status, disability and social participation was not available although much was made of estimates of travel times to units. Travel times were seen as proxies for measuring patient access and used to consider the consequences of changes in siting of units. Thinking of the extent to which the analyses undertook by the group corresponds with the components of basic needs set out by Doyal and Gough (see page 22) a number of gaps in the needs assessment work can be identified. The limits of time and resources available to the group should not be forgotten here but these gaps had a considerable consequence for the rationality of decision making for they allowed exogenous pressures to affect the decision making process. Information on survival was either insufficient or not used because it was considered too sensitive. Information on service use, in the form of acceptance rates was by far the most accurate data available to the group and this was used extensively. Even here however, the limits of the data were apparent. The review group was only able to analyse activity occurring in the NHS. Private patients were therefore excluded from the analysis. Whilst this was not considered a major problem by group members, the relationship between private practice and health sector inequity has been graphically highlighted in other specialties (Yates 1995).

There was no analysis by gender or social status and no information was available on levels of disability, patient functioning or patient's health status. The group had no information on the mental health of the renal patient or on the impact their condition had on their social networks. There was no assessment of the socio-economic impact of renal disease. The group's work therefore only covered autonomy in the sense of some comments by group members on the psycho-social impact of the condition and a general opinion that travelling long distances to treatment centres compromised the quality of life of patients. The inaccessibility of some units was highlighted and in this way improving 'access' was seen as an important component in the task of addressing 'need'.

Inequity of access became a determining factor in the construction of a technical picture of patient needs. The phrase 'equal access for equal need' seems to best describe the overall approach undertaken. Decisions were based on quantitative data showing variations in use of services (focusing on ethnicity and geography) together with the subjective opinions of group members on the impact that travelling long distances had on the lives of patients. Data on outcome and objective levels of disability were either ignored or not available. The group clearly focused on a particular interpretation of need for its work. It is more difficult to untangle the way in which this was used to inform decision making. In deciding on which units should be retained as tertiary centres the group turned to its assessment of their academic status and to judgements about their viability in the wider context of a developing market for health care in London. The main factors affecting the group's decisions therefore were:

1.   Need: epidemiologically defined and related to access to services
2.   Academic status
3.   'Market' viability

The next chapter examines the role of professional power in the needs assessment process and looks at how the three factors mentioned above interacted and affected the rationality of decision making.

Notes

1   The Tomlinson inquiry was set up in October 1991 to 'advise on the organisation of and inter-relationships between, the National Health Service and medical education and research in London'. The report recommended that 'a dedicated implementation group be set up to co-ordinate change and that it placed priority on setting up working groups to review the rationalisation of specialty provision in London' (p. 1 Tomlinson report).

2   The review group focused on renal services in the Greater London area but also considered the four Thames Regions as a whole since there was 'substantial overlap in the provision for patients throughout this area' (p. 1 renal review group report).

3   Renal replacement therapy (RRT) is given to people who are suffering from End Stage Renal Failure (ESRF). Without therapy these patients will die. The main types of treatment offered under RRT are, dialysis, haemodialysis, continuous ambulatory peritoneal dialysis and transplantation.

5 Professional power and the need for health care

Introduction

This chapter considers health needs embodied in contested professional discourses. The focus is on the extent to which professional debates concerning needs can be explained in terms of strategic action (aimed at achieving success) or communicative action (aimed at achieving consensus). With respect to the renal review discussions therefore I will ask was it possible for professional groups to make a commitment to expose ideas and arguments to collective evaluation? How did theoretical understandings of needs relate to communicative understandings? The discussion is illustrated with transcribed extracts from the review group's internal debates and minutes of meetings held with the 12 renal units in London.[1]

Meetings with renal units

In this discussion of the debates that occurred in the meetings with renal units I draw a distinction between communicative action, open strategic action and concealed strategic action. The ostensible driving force behind the discussions was the need to get issues out in the open and to allow the actors involved to participate fully. However, the extent of this participation was limited in two crucial ways; firstly by the exclusion of actors who would be affected by the debates and secondly by the extent to which powerful interests set constraints on the willingness of individuals or groups to question proposals, express their views and introduce their own proposals. The extent to which actors were excluded could be clearly seen in the limited involvement of patients and patient groups and the medical dominance of the debates. The constraining effect of powerful groups is more difficult to analyse as this may have resulted in some voices not being heard at all, whilst others may have modified or muted the tenor of their remarks. All quoted extracts in this section are taken from the minutes of the meetings with the renal units.

Definition of need and decision making criteria

Units used the meeting to present a case for them to be a future core centre. The formal arguments and evidence they employed focused on geographical access, quality of services, cost-effectiveness of services, the unit's position in the market, the unit's ability to manage change and the academic and research record of the unit. The emphasis given to each of these areas varied from unit to unit. This depended on two main factors: a) the unit's perception of where its main strengths lay and b) the unit's perception of what factors the renal review group would base its decision on, the relative weight it would give to geographic access vis-à-vis academic excellence for example. The St Bartholomew's unit placed considerable emphasis on geographic access:

> All agreed that dialysis needed to be devolved closer to patient homes.

But they tempered this with evidence on the needs of patients in their immediate area:

> Hackney is an extremely deprived area and it was felt that moving the dialysis unit away from Barts could add to their disadvantage.

These statements reveal the strong link made between patient needs and geographic access and an acceptance that service provision in London would have to change to address these needs. However, in order to justify arguments for the Bart's unit's continued existence there was an equally strong emphasis on the need of local populations where needs were linked to levels of relative deprivation. The renal review group's emphasis on restructuring services in order to make them more appropriate to patient needs was not being disputed, but there was a strong appeal to the link between deprivation and increasing need for renal services to add force to arguments in favour of the unit being retained. These arguments can be contrasted with the renal review group's working definition of need which did not make such a link. Although the review group had made a clear definition of epidemiological need, it was clear that the ambivalence that still surrounded the term 'patient needs' still allowed it to be manipulated to legitimate particular arguments and interests. In this sense the need for renal services was still a contested concept.

Most units regarded the arguments linking patient needs to geographic access (based on evidence showing the remoteness of services and underprovision in certain areas) as indisputable. The review group's presentation of a model for future provision based on these arguments was generally accepted. The focus for disputes therefore was the selection of which units should form the core. The main decision making criteria for selecting units was considered to be the research and academic record of a unit. The damage that shifting units around could do to their respective research potential was often cited as an argument for staff to remain on their existing sites, and units spent considerable time outlining their research output and future research plans. As time went by it became increasingly apparent that a pecking order was forming in terms of each unit's relative research and academic status. Those units lower down this pecking order and in competition with the high status units, were more likely to emphasise their strengths in meeting patient needs as well as the cost-effectiveness and quality of their services. It was possible to distinguish between units that were perceived by the group, and by the units themselves, to be of high academic and research standards, and units that were considered to be of a lesser standard but often with a good record in providing a renal service. Some units were strong in both areas of course and this gave them a considerable advantage in that they could play the 'patient need' and the 'academic record' with equal effect in their negotiations with the review group. Nevertheless, there often seemed to be confusion within units about which strengths to play to. At St Thomas' for example the emphasis was placed on the potential for future research:

> [W] added that the judgmental value should bear in mind
> the potential of units for research.

but this statement, although mainly concerned with how research should be judged is immediately followed by a statement emphasising another decision making criteria:

> [J] argued that service provision should be the major
> determining factor.

The St Thomas' clinicians seemed to be able to jump from needs/service based arguments to arguments concerning future research with ease. Indeed, if they saw conflict between the two they were very careful not to show it. This perhaps reflected the unit's ability to demonstrate strengths in both areas whilst recognising the need for improvement. These arguments were presented to the group by the St Thomas' team in a friendly, non-confrontational, manner where there appeared to be a good deal of understanding between clinicians on the review group and the hospital clinicians. Clearly it was important for the St Thomas' team to set out a strong academic and service case. It would be wrong however to interpret this in Habermasian terms as a form of 'action oriented towards understanding', since some interests were excluded at the time of the debate; most notably the patients and their representatives. This highlights the importance of Habermas' point that the validity of any claim is subject to the consensus of those affected by the claim. The structure of the review group's meetings meant that interested parties were inevitably excluded from certain debates. These included the public, renal patients, NHS staff and consultants in other units. Given the practical difficulties of undertaking a review of this sort, it would be impossible to involve all interested parties in the debate. Of course Habermas' concept of communicative understanding is an ideal type of communication. Nevertheless, it is possible to criticise the review process in relation to how much it endeavoured to ensure open and fair debate. There was no formal mechanism for the minutes of meetings with the group to be circulated among every unit in London for example. In light of this the statements made in the minutes must be seen primarily as elites taking up negotiating positions and as forms of strategic action. In the case of the St Thomas' team, their negotiating position was very strong and they could therefore afford to be generous in their statements. This was reflected in the comparatively relaxed atmosphere of the St Thomas' unit. At the Royal Free hospital, on the other hand, tension between academic criteria and patient needs could not be so easily reconciled and the unit questioned how:

> comparisons could be made between academic research and patient care as a basis for the review group's decision making.

The Royal Free was a unit where the review group's deliberations were seen much more as a threat to the unit's future. The unit had emphasised the high quality of its service, its cost effectiveness relative to other London units and its accessibility to patients. The possibility of losing out to a judgement that gave too much weight to 'academic' status at the expense of the above qualities was therefore a considerable concern. This can be contrasted with the arguments presented in favour of the St Peter's unit at University College Hospital where:

The primary reason given was the academic and research base for nephrology at St Peter's. These were believed to be real, tangible and important. Progress in clinical management was dependent on such a base.

The emphasis here was on the research and academic excellence of the hospital as a whole and for the renal unit:

> it would not make sense to be separated from it, despite some problems of access for patients.

Here we clearly see precedence being given to academic status over patient access, by a unit confident in the strengths of its research and academic position and the impact that would have on the renal review group's judgement.

'Need' was most frequently spoken of in the context of access to services. This was formulated in terms of patients not receiving treatment because not enough services were available, and in terms of the distances patients had to travel to units. The first part of this formulation was used to buttress arguments that services had to be protected and even expanded in the face of calls for rationalisation. The later part was used to highlight the remoteness of London units from patient populations and the consequent need for relocation of services. There was a general recognition that services were inappropriately located and had not developed in a manner that addressed patient needs. However, beyond this shared understanding there was plenty of scope for disagreement and debate concerning which services should be rationalised and which should be developed. Relating this to Doyal and Gough's rules for discussing needs it is clear that these debates were a threat to any attempt to address need satisfaction. The group was not only looking at the need for services in the population but also at how services could be reconfigured in a way that ensured the future of London units as 'centres of excellence'. This suggests that the group's discussion on needs corresponded with 'expert needs talk' (Fraser 1989). This refers to 'needs talk' that can perpetuate professional class formation, provide a platform for defusing political conflict in relation to needs and can be understood as forms of social problem solving. This in turn meant that the basis for discussing future service provision and the criteria on which decisions were to be based were clearly contestable concepts. By emphasising the importance of academic excellence above all other criteria as a means of securing their own survival, units were engaged in strategic action. This could be interpreted as open strategic action because the intention to influence the review process was openly declared. However, looking at the ways in which the arguments were presented it is also possible that processes of unconscious self-deception were also at work in that the justification for maintaining academic excellence stemmed from a highly medicalised perspective. From the viewpoint of the medical elites it is not surprising that patient needs appeared secondary to research interests.

Markets

The potential the market had for affecting radically the plans of the various interests involved, was a source of considerable concern. There was a realisation that not every unit stood in the same position relative to the market, and this generated levels of uncertainty. To understand how this uncertainty affected the negotiations taking place it is important to grasp the way in which the various factional interests interacted. The different renal units could be seen as a set of interest groups, vying with one another to be chosen as a specialist centre. Managers, nurses and medics within each unit generally presented a united front in support of the unit. On the other hand, there were also divisions between professional groupings particularly medics and managers. These divisions could work across unit loyalties and were discernible in the way in which managers and medics reacted to the review group's suggestions; managers demonstrating a much greater willingness to accept the fundamental need for rationalising services and the perceived inevitability of the Tomlinson proposals, while medics were more likely to challenge the assumptions behind the review group's remit. The market therefore was seen to have the capacity to determine the 'winners' and 'losers' in this process as far as renal units were concerned. However, the levels of uncertainty produced by this, created opportunities for managers, as an interest group, to increase their influence over matters and remind medics of the rationalising imperative driving the whole process.

The relative strengths and position of units in the market was debated time and time again. This had particular relevance to the Hammersmith hospital which had Special Health Authority (SHA) status. Being an SHA meant that the unit could not yet compete in the market and its services were paid for directly from central funds thus making them an attractive zero price service for local purchasers. The Hammersmith physicians, when criticised for not developing dialysis services in response to patient needs, countered with the argument that their SHA status had not given them the freedom to do this:

> The team also felt that they had been constrained by the
> market. Purchasers have treated the Hammersmith as a free
> good.

Implicit in this was the belief that if the Hammersmith team were allowed to enter the market then they could attract the necessary funds to allow them to expand services. While they were seen as a free good however there was no incentive to do this. The chair of the review group saw this as an opportunity to state that if the unit was to be allowed to enter the market, in order to survive in the market it would have to expand its renal programme to address patient needs. Here the market was being used as a threat. This argument was accepted but concerns were raised about the effect this would have on the academic workload of the unit that was seen as its greatest strength. These concerns, which in turn had a feeling of a veiled threat about them, were swiftly countered with the chair of the review group stating that he:

> recognised these concerns but added that the reality of the market may force the unit to dilute the purity of its academic position.

This shows the duality of market based arguments. The market could be utilised by a unit to support its case but there was also a danger in such a strategy for the same market based arguments to be turned back against the unit by the chair of the review group. The perceived danger of the market for prestige academic units can be clearly seen here. The weakness of a 'centre of academic excellence' such as the Hammersmith could easily be exploited and its neighbouring unit, Charing Cross, leapt at the opportunity in its meeting with the review group to state:

> The Hammersmith may not have fully grasped the consequences of becoming a DGH within the market...the interdependencies that Charing Cross had built up in the area made them a strong player in the market.

Although the medics in the units were clearly aware of these arguments and frequently alluded to them, it was noticeable that the managers involved (the chief executives and financial managers) were more likely to vocalise such arguments. There was a general awareness of what the market meant for individual units in terms of threats and opportunities. When this was translated into the implications for London as a whole, the potential the market had for forcing the pace of change was not underestimated by clinicians and managers at the Guy's unit:

> DHAs had not attempted to play units against each other yet, though clearly their view is that there are too many units at present. It was generally accepted that purchasers will be able to push for rationalisation.

There was a strong belief in the ability of purchasers to use the market to rationalise services. There was a marked split in the attitude of managers and doctors towards the market. The former were more likely to perceive the market as something positive that was driven by patient needs. The latter were more prone to see the market as a potential source of chaos. No one produced any evidence of the market's capacity to do these things. In this sense, when individuals spoke about the market they were referring to something abstract: an idea of the market. If we take Habermas' distinction between the objective world, the social world and the subjective world, the abstract nature of the market becomes problematic because it was used by the speakers to justify their notion of changes to the objective world. Their perception of the market however was drawn from their subjective world experiences and from the social world of interpersonal relationships. This highlights the ways in which the market is socially embedded but was portrayed as something of the objective world. The importance of this characteristic of the market is that it then becomes a powerful argumentative device because it is seen to represent something about the world that has a claim to truth.

It is interesting to contrast the perceived role of the market with the perceived role of the renal review group. One of the main reasons for setting up the specialty review groups was to manage the market; to minimise the potential chaos the market could create. The group's task in writing an independent review of renal services was to draw up a set of recommendations for future provision of services. Such an objective might be seen in terms of an exercise in traditional 'rational' planning but the realisation that such a plan would ultimately be tested in the market place meant that it would be impossible for the group to indulge in 'classical planning' in the face of market imperatives. This created an ambivalence in the minds of renal review group members and representatives in the units. At King's for example:

> [E] asked how the centre could ensure that the periphery retained their original function and did not expand their services to include transplant for example. [M] added that this was a crucial question for the London Implementation Group (LIG) because of the interface between LIG's planning role and the role of the market.

This question was never resolved either within the group or outside it. From the point of view of the meetings with the renal units, what is interesting is that some clinicians in the units did see the review group as having the potential to counter the threat from the market. For example at Guy's:

[L] argued that the breakdown of Regions contributed to planning blight and saw this exercise as an opportunity to reintroduce some planning.

These sentiments were echoed by those units who emphasised their research status and can be contrasted with the views of those units who were happier to see their future being determined by the market. To reconcile the review group's planning role with the introduction of the market requires a perception of the group as an attempt to manage markets. The meetings with the units were settings for debates between powerful vested interests and the minutes of these meetings document the manner in which these vested interests were confronted with, and responded to, the prospect of the market. Whilst managers remained fairly silent during the debates on patient needs and the research status of units, seeing this as the domain of the medics, they were quick to engage in debates concerning the market. This reflects the extent to which managers saw discussions about 'the market' as part of their domain; somewhere where their expertise and knowledge could influence debate. Managers therefore contributed to debates by using 'the market' as a platform for strategic action. There were important differences in the way the market was interpreted by managers and doctors. Despite the fact that there was no clear understanding of what 'the market' stood for, the existence of 'the market' was not questioned because, however it was defined, the term had a social currency that allowed it to be used to support the agendas of particular groups.

Power and vested interests

The operation of power and the protection of vested interests was most visible in the way the review group addressed the future of academic units in relation to the restructuring of medical schools in London. In the South Western sector, medical school support played a crucial role in determining the choice of St George's hospital over St Helier; so much so that the Dean of the medical school:

> stated that the medical school did not believe that the academic developments could be centred on the St Helier site.

In the North and the North East, the possible future configuration of medical schools and hospitals made the situation particularly complex. In order to facilitate decision making, the chair of the review group pressed at every meeting for a clear statement from medical school representatives on the units they planned to be linked with in the future. In light of this, the relationship between medical school representatives and the renal unit representatives was difficult to untangle. A medical school representative attending a meeting between the review group and a unit linked to the medical school may have given verbal support to that unit, knowing that the medical school's future lay elsewhere. This meant that the chair of the review group found it difficult to tie the representatives down to a confirmatory statement at the formal meetings but instead would often opt for an agreement from the medical school to give a statement in writing.

This strategy released the representatives from the difficult task of making statements in the presence of colleagues most likely to be affected by them, thus saving face, whilst at the same time tied them down to making a commitment to giving a written statement to the renal review group. This shows how the discussions with the renal units, whilst giving the appearance of free and open debate, contained layers of concealed views and hidden agendas. The strategy of the chair was to try to reveal the 'true' agendas of the actors involved, without causing or threatening the kind of embarrassment in front of colleagues that would result in such views becoming more difficult to gather. This meant that some negotiations and meetings were inevitably conducted outside the formal consultation process of the review. Between the review group's members there was a recognition that discussion outside of the review group's formal process would be necessary and that these discussions were vital if potential conflicts were to be defused:

> Requests had been made by medical bodies for prior sights of [the group's] draft report; these would be refused, but it might be helpful to hold confidential discussion later. (minutes of internal review group meeting)

This did not mean that all the group members approved of this but it was impossible not to be aware of this aspect of the review process, as the chair would regularly update group members on the outside discussions he and others had been having. In this sense there was no concealment of a strategy to influence matters outside of the group. Given the nature of some of the discussions and the medical elites involved, it would have been surprising if this had not been happening. Relating this to the tension between understandings of power and the formal rules for an ideal speech situation; the compulsion not to speak openly in the debates often manifested itself in the form of self censorship by the powerful, who saw opportunities to indulge in forms of strategic action outside of the formal review process. This can be related to Lukes' second face of power and shows how the character of the debates could be compromised by the co-production of power.

Conclusion

The meetings of the review group with units were presented as an opportunity for a fair, open and democratic debate on the issues. However, the exclusion of some groups and the conduct of negotiations outside the meetings meant that the impression of fairness and clarity of debate given in the minutes was illusory. The idea of having gone through the process of consulting the units and allowing them to have their say could be seen more as a cathartic exercise than an attempt to open debate. On the other hand, the entrenched institutional and professional loyalties of unit representatives also stifled any discussion of service need. The combination of these forces meant that the desire to minimise conflict acted to dampen debate.

The renal review group working meetings

This section interrogates the tapes of the review group working meetings held at the Department of Health. All of the review group members attended the meetings and a number of finance managers, researchers and academics also attended to give specialist advice. Apart from the chair (T) individuals are only identified by a code representing their status (C=Clinician, M=Manager, A=Academic, N=Nurse).[2] In some parts of the analysis quotations from the transcribed tapes are presented in conjunction with the relevant extracts from the minutes of the meetings; the tapes are printed in ordinary font whilst minutes are printed in italic. This allows the discussions of the group to be contrasted with the formal record and throws light on how the discussions were used to manufacture a coherent plan of future services.

A model for renal services

As we have seen, the group's brief was to come up with a model of future renal service provision across London. This was being done against a backdrop of expectations of considerable rationalisation in the capital and considerable uncertainty as to the effect of health care markets in the future. The group's chairman was therefore concerned that the model the group came up with was acceptable to as many people as possible, particularly the clinicians, some of whom could possibly lose their power base because of it. It is therefore significant that at only the second internal meeting of the review group, before the review process had been undertaken, the minutes concluded with the following statement:

Preliminary conclusions on tertiary centres
The Steering Group noted that London fell naturally into five sectors. In the South East, the merger of Guy's and St Thomas' was already agreed, and the Group considered that this unit's strength left King's as a weak contender for renal services in this sector. In the North East the Royal London, perhaps merged with Bart's was the obvious site. In the South West, there was only one academic unit - St George's - despite the wish of St Helier for separation. St George's strength as a cardiac unit made it the obvious choice for renal services. In the North/centre, University College Middlesex had the best academic and scientific base in London. In the West, Hammersmith too was the outstanding performer. The Chairman reported that this overview was consistent with the emerging views of the Cardiac and Neurosciences group.

This extract highlights a number of important points. Firstly, it shows how the planning process of the review was constrained from the outset by the concept of five geographical sectors for London's specialist health services. Secondly, it demonstrates the extent to which the possible recommendations of other review group's (Cardiac and Neurosciences) influenced the decision making processes of the renal review. Thirdly, and most importantly, it shows that not only was the model for future provision defined in the first meetings of the review group, but the five specialist centres were also identified very clearly. The above statement is almost identical to the final recommendations of the review group report. This suggests that the review process itself was less a means of arriving at a set of health care decisions and more a means of legitimising decisions that had, more or less, already been taken.

Getting agreement on the proposed model as early as possible formed the foundation of the review Chair's strategy. This meant ensuring all the group members were committed to the proposed model and there was no likelihood of dissent at any part of the process (particularly when group members were visiting units). From the transcribed tapes of the same meeting it is possible to see the importance given to this:

T   Now I, I, I, don't want to end up within the group with conflict on this issue that would mean chaos really and I, I, I think we need just to have it out so that people understand what we're talking about and if anybody has questions or views let's have them now.

The chair made it clear that the group was free to, and indeed should, debate the relative merits of the different units, but there had to be a commitment to the model from the outset. The operation of power is clear here and the tone of the statement implies disapproval of any questioning, doubt or scepticism as far as the model is concerned. This does not mean that individuals could not voice doubts within the group, but it clearly meant that those doubts could no longer be openly and formally expressed as part of the review group's dealing with the units. The fullness of the participation of review group members in the debate was thus immediately placed in jeopardy. Indeed, it was difficult for anyone to raise questions or proposals concerning the model subsequent to this event. The freedom of members to question any proposal or introduce any proposal into the discourse was constrained by the chair's statement.

The proposed model focused on five teaching units based in central units with autonomous non-teaching units on the periphery of the Thames Regions, and smaller units in between providing basic dialysis care. The group spent a good deal of time and energy discussing how these different types of units could be described in the model and a whole host of terms including secondary, tertiary, teaching, primary, satellite were used, discarded and returned to again and again.

T I think if we were just to say autonomous centres and centres which look to other centres, somewhere else for support, that might be sufficient.

C5 The use of the word secondary and tertiary confuses it rather. We must use secondary, if we use it at all, for those centres which have two to three nephrologists able to do the work.

T Looking at this green book here M2 you've got a facility for words, what term should we use?

M2 I must admit I'm still a little unclear about what we're griping at with autonomous and secondary so I'm not yet in a position to do the words.

T Well can I reiterate then. An autonomous centre is one which carries out all the foreseeable functions a nephrology centre should carry out with one exception and that is transplantation.

M2 Got that.

C4 I would call that a secondary centre.

C2 Can I just say that we'd prefer not primary because of its connotations with primary care.

M2 So we've got autonomous centres which,

T We've got University centres.

M2   Oh sorry yes right, the University centres, then autonomous centres which have full scale nephrologist cover on site.

T   Why can't we just call them nephrology centres?

M2   OK and they do all the things you'd expect a nephrological centre to do except transplants. I, I, I, can grasp that, Emmm ...(1.5) I'm not sure I like the lesser centres.

C5   Well I,

C2   We used to call them subsidiary centres but ehmm,

M2   Hence the word satellite or is satellite one yet again?

T   No, satellite might cover it. It has different connotations which is helpful...

These debates were often quite frustrating for those involved, and sometimes bordered on the farcical, but the semantics involved were a crucial part of the group's work. Using the three phases of depth hermeneutics it is important to remind ourselves of the social context for these debates. Specialist services in London were under pressure to rationalise because of oversupply, uncoordinated supply and poorly planned supply. If these criticisms were to be addressed, then inevitably some prestigious teaching centres would be under threat. The model for future renal services proposed by the group had to make a distinction between the teaching centres that would survive the shake up, and those centres that could no longer be described as teaching centres. There was also a need to identify the continuing function of these non-teaching centres (assuming the hospitals themselves did not close). Finally, in line with the perceived need to expand services into geographic areas where people were not receiving treatment, the idea of smaller units had to be clearly defined. Against the background of trying to reconcile competing claims of increasing provision to meet unmet need, the need to preserve teaching centres and the need to rationalise services; the importance of agreeing clear definitions of services becomes apparent.

The definitional problems seem to centre on the need to distinguish between units in a hierarchical sense without introducing terms that could be construed as demeaning to a unit. Terms such as 'secondary', 'subsidiary' and 'lesser' were introduced but were clearly unacceptable. Here we see a sensitivity to the cultural consequences of changes in service levels. The importance of this nomenclature becomes apparent if we consider its possible effects on the responses by London's renal physicians to the review group's proposed changes.

In analysing the tape extract, it is significant that the discussion was mainly conducted between the chair of the group and one of the managers on the group. The contributions of other members were peripheral to the main thrust of this debate, which was to instil in all group members, but particularly managers, a commitment to a three tiered hierarchy of renal units. A look at how this debate was recorded in the minutes of the meeting shows how this commitment was formalised:

> It was agreed that there were three levels of renal unit:
>
> University transplant centre - the five London centres already tentatively identified, providing all renal services
>
> Autonomous renal unit - having resident nephrologist(s) and substantially all services except transplantation
>
> Satellite unit - linked to one of the higher units providing routine dialysis and outpatient clinics as needed.
> (Internal review group meeting 1st April 1993)

The apparent ambivalence of the manager in the taped extract towards the distinction between the words 'autonomous, 'secondary' and 'satellite' reflects an overall ambivalence towards the construction of a 'blueprint' for London's services. The minutes gave these concepts a clarity and legitimacy that was missing from the debates. The construction of an elegant model for future services does not therefore appear to have arisen from the review group's work. Instead its genesis was external to the review and it was brought to the group for confirmation by the Chair.

In many respects, apart from the siting of the five teaching centres, the group shied away from specifying where other smaller units should be sited and although the group discussed possible sites for smaller units, the large units themselves were encouraged to come up with solutions to this problem. This issue was brought up when the group visited different units, but the issue was also discussed outside official group meetings between the clinicians on the group and the clinicians in the units.

T   now Canterbury, I have debated that with the Guy's unit already and they feel that it is probably, despite its apparent geographical isolation, probably a place where further developments could take place, it's already a fully established service of course.

It is interesting to note that Canterbury is seen as 'geographically isolated', perhaps reflecting the London focus of the review rather than an understanding of the geographical location of Canterbury. In addition, the passage gives an indication of the extent to which the units outside London came under (or at least was seen to be under) the sphere of influence of

London's clinicians. The statement hints at the kind of informal negotiations that were being carried on outside the group, but also highlights the Chair's concern to keep group members informed of what was going on and to bring these issues back to the group for confirmation. There may have been instances where the Chair chose not to inform the group of certain discussions, but his strategy at all times was to ensure that the final report had the full agreement of group members. Making group members feel that they were engaged in all debates was an important part of this strategy. This could be interpreted as a search for consensus, but the need to placate those who were excluded from these behind the scenes negotiations was also a factor. Some of course were not placated, and notes of these meetings indicate that there were instances where individuals voiced, in private, some concerns about the nature of informal discussion. There was a clear division between doctors and managers in this respect, with both set of stakeholders engaging in outside discussions among their own peers. Academics, nurses and patient representatives were, in the main, excluded from this and in informal discussions would frequently question the process, often taking the opportunity to make jokes about their 'subordinate role' or the deliberations of the 'great and the good'. Many of the discussions held within the group therefore may have appeared to be open and democratic and of being oriented towards understanding, but exclusions (most notably of renal patients) and restrictions within the group itself, ensured that the debates were 'closed', undemocratic and oriented towards strategic action. It is of course easier to maintain the illusion of openness where the possibility of challenge and conflict is minimised.

Definition of need

Need was based on the figure of 80 new patients per million population per annum and there was evidence of considerable geographic variations in access to services depending on age, ethnicity and proximity to services. This prompted considerable debate among group members as to how the 'unmet need' and the inequity that they had identified could be addressed, and whether they could relate this to other debates they were having about the cost and cost effectiveness of renal services, the balance between population needs and the need to protect academic interests:

A1   There's one other thing which is a long term issue which we perhaps come to, there's evidence that the more renal units you have the higher the referral rate becomes.

(Laughter)

I mean one of the things, although the London system is by no means planned, it is a highly effective safety valve or rationing device because centres are so relatively inaccessible and poorly sited and we have, ehm, people have to realise that one of the consequences of Tomlinson renal service distribution is going to be much greater pressure on GPs and General Physicians, now whether that 'you ain't seen nothing yet' could be one motto they have to warn people that they are, that from decentralising provision in other countries, it does lead to much greater problems of high extra demand, you've been able to keep a lid on expansion by reminding Guy's, Barts and the London to provide a service so ehm,

T   But it's so unequal you see South West Thames and North East Thames, North West Thames and South East it's very low.

A1   Well that's their problem isn't it.

C5   No, No, after all there are people there. I mean we know from our studies, eh, that somewhere between 70 and 80 new patients a year would be produced from the population that is there. So we have to plan for the population that's there, not what it has come to before, and eh, moving the sites is not going to reduce the patients, they're there, they're not imaginary.

T   Yes that's a nice way of putting it.

This excerpt reveals a tension between the resource implications of defining 'need' at levels above those being met by present services and the moral implications of people not receiving care they 'need' because of geographic inequity. The statement referring to the levels of services provision under the existing London system as an 'effective safety valve' is important because it highlights the dilemmas arising from calls to make the system more responsive to need when by being unresponsive the system had functioned efficiently as a rationing device. Thus the conflicts between a government policy aimed at meeting needs and government policy aimed at controlling public expenditure are thrown into stark relief. Although the group never resolved the conflict between limited resources and unmet need (they would return to this issue on a number of occasions), the baseline need figure of 80 new patients per million served as an ultimate appeal to an absolute level of need in the case of disputes. The clinicians on the group focused on the inequity of provision and the unmet need that the epidemiological work had highlighted. There seemed to be two factors at work here: a genuine concern that people were not receiving treatment and were therefore dying unnecessarily and an opportunity to focus on arguments for an expansion in service provision as a balance to the Tomlinson report's drive for rationalisation. There were concerns however that the idea of 'unmet need' could represent a moveable feast characterised by regular shifts in the threshold for need. Clearly these ideas were underpinned by the concept of infinite demand and there was some suspicion as to the absolute nature of the clinician's figure of 80 new patients per million per year. Nevertheless, the epidemiological arguments held sway.

The academic here (A1) was trying to introduce a proposal into the group's discussion; that of rationing by means of controlling the quantity of supply, the location of supply and public expectations. The laughter from group members following the academic's first statement is a sign that they were aware of these issues. It is interesting that the managers present did not follow the academic's lead and challenge the implicit assumption that services needed to expand. The clinicians on the group on the other hand were quick to respond by claiming the moral high ground of 'unmet need'. Not only does this emphasise the importance given to the epidemiological definition of need, but more importantly we see that the ownership of the definition was clearly in the medical domain and was very difficult to challenge. This is apparent in the way the debate appears to abate after C5's somewhat crude summary of the epidemiological evidence. What seems to evolve from this is the idea of a medical paradigm of need that acts as a major controlling mechanism for the group's debates. This paradigm of need can be related to Habermas' three stage validity analysis where the validity of a statement is justified by claims of truth (concerning the objective world), claims of rightness (concerning the shared world) or claims of truthfulness (concerning the subjective world). The definition of need seemed to be presented as a claim to truth (saying something about the objective world). However, the academic on the group revealed the subjective elements to the definition of need. It is clearly a social construct and is concerned with the shared world. It is a normative claim that can be challenged and defended on a number of levels. The lack of debate concerning this paradigm of need, together with its apparent use as an objective claim to truth, suggests that it possessed a social currency that allowed the clinicians on the group to avoid having to justify its validity.

Economic arguments (costs)

The group spent a considerable amount of time discussing the costs of renal replacement therapy. Part of this discussion focused on patient transport costs. There was concern, particularly among the clinicians on the group that patient travel times were not only a cost to patients themselves but a drain on NHS resources:

T   That's 90 minutes a day, three times a week and that's just travelling time let alone the waiting time, so you are looking at very large costs. How can we get at that M2 have you any idea?

M2   I don't think we should.

T   Eh, right OK.

M2   I think our job, is certainly to take a view on the proper level of accessibility and it may well be that our view is that many places are unacceptably inaccessible, if you see what I mean, ehm but having done that the principle in the rules of the game is that patients find their way to reasonably accessible units and that's their affair. There are costs of course for people who can't, you know, there are special you know low income provision and all that sort of thing.

T   So we don't, I mean you could take, do have to point out the cost of not having satellite units. I mean there is a profound negative cost in having sixty percent of your maintenance patients travelling by hospital car or ambulance.

C8   It could be quite important. I would really say if we're actually saying we're going to have more elderly patients on dialysis, one model is to have more hospital based dialysis that's accessible. It's going to be such an NHS transport cost if the elderly are actually going to require an ambulance or a hospital car to get up two or three times a week.

M2   Ehm, where there is an inescapable cost on the NHS then we should be taking account of it but I don't think, eh we should not be doing some macro department of transport style, you know we saved the van driver four minutes at the by-pass.

T   Right, yes fine.

N   Just to say though that over the years the transport costs have gone up of course. Because of the elderly patient because technology's improved, we're treating more sick people who can't make it under their own steam. So if we're saying that the population is going to increase, is going to double over the next seven years, so will transport costs.

101

This interchange reveals some tension within the group as to the extent of its remit. Managers were conscious of their need to ensure that the group kept to a prescribed task and did not stray too far away from its main aims. The short time scale for the group's work was often cited to back this up. In discussing transport costs there was a danger that the group became too involved in the wider social implications of their investigations. The argument that the group should only concentrate on NHS costs was therefore strongly pushed by the managers on the group at this point. Relating this to the aims of the group, one of which was to assess patient needs, it is clear that managers may have been content to accept a medicalised definition of need but were opposed to any attempt to broaden the analysis of needs and quickly stifled any thoughts of looking at the impact of travel costs on individual patients.

The manager on this debate emphasised the role of taking a view on the 'proper level of accessibility'. This suggests that the role of the group as one of 'taking a view' on matters, recording the wisdom of the 'great and the good' or documenting the opinions of elites was acceptable to managers. They were however less comfortable with the notion of the group becoming enthusiastic about its remit and looking at the evidence for needs in greater detail, particularly when this seemed to involve straying into the territory beyond the immediate responsibility of the health service. The managers were therefore keen to set limits to the concept of 'accessibility' used by the group. Their success in doing this stems, in part, from the inadequate basis for discussing the relationship between 'need' and 'access'. Without a clear understanding of how these issues should be discussed they were subject to the problems of contrasting and conflicting definitions. In other words the framework for debate was sufficiently malleable to allow managers to renege on the concept of accessibility. In response to the manager's statement, the clinicians seemed to modify their approach to set out the impact of an increasingly elderly population, that is remote from service centres, on direct health service costs such as hospital cars and ambulances. This was then re-interpreted by the manager in terms of looking at 'inescapable costs' to the NHS. This reveals the ways in which costs and needs can be captured by the perspective of the actors discussing them. Given their brief, the managers were right to remind the group that this was a review of health services. However the distinction between health service and non-health service costs becomes blurred when the kind of issues raised by the nurse in the debate are considered. It is this blurring that the managers on the group wished to avoid. Nevertheless the review did estimate that savings of about £550,000 would accrue from providing satellite units closer to patients and that these savings would 'rise to between

£1.6 million and £1.8 million for a full steady state haemodialysis population', (Renal Review Report Appendix D, p. 13).

The clinicians, managers and academics on the group found it more difficult to resolve the contentious issue of the cost-effectiveness of renal services. This was due to the clinicians on the group contesting the view that CAPD was more cost-effective than hospital haemodialysis.

A1   Well, yeh I mean, unless we understated the full cost of CAPD and I understand some studies did then obviously ...we're talking about a very much less cost-effective service at the margin and that is something, I mean although you said that quality wasn't an issue for the group I mean cost-effectiveness is something some of the purchasers are going to be concerned about. I mean we may not have the perfect set of research studies unfortunately but the existing literature is very very clear that if people have the choice then of course CAPD is being pursued at a national level but it happens for a wide spectrum of patients to be more cost-effective that's not to say it's ideal for any one individual patient but at a service level because of the differences in cost...

C7   No, I think the costs are narrowing because people are aware that in fact it isn't cheaper and in fact what wasn't being costed before is now being costed.

T   The hidden costs are coming out.

C7   The hidden costs are coming out and I think the fact is as we mentioned earlier; you can't have a CAPD programme without having a haemodialysis back up. It's not possible.

The clinicians were not disputing the need for cost-effectiveness analysis in health care, rather they were questioning the technical basis for the cost-effectiveness studies that had been undertaken in the past. They were in fact keen to get good cost-effectiveness data into the report but clearly this had to be done on their terms. Their terms included a severe criticism of previous cost comparisons of different treatment options and an insistence that the interdependence of different forms of treatment be given more recognition in cost calculations. The debate reveals some of the tensions and conflicts between a national policy of promoting CAPD as a treatment option, individual patient needs and a need to maintain 'viable' renal replacement therapy units. The clinician (C7) was making an important point about the weakness of previous economic evaluations, but the opportunity to widen the debate to consider the appropriate balance of treatment options to meet patient needs was lost by the urgency of the need to criticise cost

103

calculations. It is here that the strength of the clinicians on the group is most apparent for they were able to direct the debates concerning the cost of renal services. Managers were largely passive, leaving the discussions to the academics involved. Given that these discussions dealt with the factors that could determine the cost and structure of future services this is initially surprising, but it became increasingly apparent that the managers on the group were more concerned with controlling the working parameters and ensuring the group kept to the timetable for producing a report. They seemed to have a jaded attitude to the review and often betrayed a sense of scepticism towards the planning process, seeing it as somewhat passé in the brave new world of purchasing and contracting. This is not to say that they failed to engage in the issues being considered by the group. Rather they seemed to see their role as one of keeping the groups discussions 'on the right track'. This being to produce proposals that conformed with the agendas for rationalising services in London. One of the ways in which they tried to do this was by reminding group members that the NHS now had a market.

Decision making criteria

Although the baseline need figure acted as a gold standard it was not the sole criteria used for planning services. The review was dealing with a large number of specialist teaching hospitals, and the preservation of teaching and research excellence in the face of the Tomlinson recommendations was an important consideration, particularly for the clinicians on the group. A dual basis for decision making was quickly established based on geographic need and academic excellence. This decision was not questioned by group members to any great extent and the managers on the group did not challenge the physicians in any way on this.

T   I should say this is unique to our specialty at the moment there's an opportunity because renal disease is historically a very academic specialty in medicine over many years much longer than renal replacement therapy has been around and of course it is now re-emerging with one of the major chairs in medicine going to a nephrologist, we are therefore going to be left with five centres picked on geographical and academic excellence, which we can look at fairly carefully, and I think that's not too difficult in the end I think to justify.

This statement reveals a strategy of appealing to the academic status of renal medicine to buttress the decision making criteria of the review group. The clear intention was to provide a cement for the legitimacy of the geographical and academic approach by reference to the elite status of a powerful medical specialty. There was however an additional facet to this strategy and that was the need to move away from need based arguments (concerning the formation of the model for renal services) to arguments about academic excellence (determining the choice of specialist units).

It is interesting to examine the above statement, in the context of what was agreed at the group's meeting to discuss the research status of the units. The minutes of the meeting begin by stating:

> The main principle guiding the renal review is that of population need. However, the need to take account of the academic profile of London units was particularly important for renal units. (Research meeting p. 1)

Following this statement, the whole of the meeting was then dedicated to discussing the relative academic merits of each London unit on a sector by sector basis. Once the issue became one of deciding the future of individual units, then 'epidemiological need' gave way to arguments about academic excellence. The criteria for assessing academic excellence relied on the value judgements of the individuals involved in the research meeting. These included research advisors from the Wellcome Trust, the Medical Research Council and the University of Cambridge. They were asked to discuss, in turn, the five geographic sectors of London. Their views on the academic status of units were to be based on publication records, grant records, scores in the University grading exercise and their own subjective estimate of a unit's position relative to others. The need for sensitivity and secrecy was a notable feature of these discussions, as was the barely concealed loyalty of some group members to units with whom they had historical links.

The debates concerning the North Western sector are interesting because they focused on the choice between the Hammersmith (a centre of academic excellence) and the Charing Cross (a centre with an impressive record of service quality). The group considered a compromise of a split site option keeping the Hammersmith and the Charing Cross units open. This was questioned by the academic advisers:

> [A2] believed that a split site option with academic activity at RPMS [The Hammersmith] and clinical activity at Charing Cross would cause difficulties ('separating the brain from the body'). (Research meeting p. 5)

This gives us an idea of how these issues were perceived by research advisors, particularly the distinction between a centre of academic excellence (the brain) and a unit with a high service workload and good quality (the body). It should not be surprising therefore to find the following view expressed:

> RPMS [Hammersmith] had several academics of international standing and a number of junior staff who had the potential to be so. The academic arguments were therefore 'cut and dried'.
> (Research meeting p. 4)

Given the force with which these arguments were made, and the emphasis given by the Chair of the group to the views of the academic advisors, it is easier to understand the confidence expressed in the quoted extract, in the group's ability to justify its decisions. The process was clearly not driven by a desire to develop shared understandings of decision making criteria. Rather it can be firmly placed in the realm of strategic action. The transparency of this strategy meant that group members became aware that this was an opportunity to influence the decision making process, if they so wished

At this point it is important to note that justifying decisions is not the same as ensuring their implementation. This may help to account for the lack of management involvement in this debate. They were aware that the likelihood of implementation of the review group's recommendations would be largely governed by the tension between the central government's response and the developing market in health care. The five centres were to be based in five geographic sectors that had been set out in the Tomlinson report. What is interesting is that no one questioned the reasoning behind the geography of these sectors. They were accepted as a given. This highlights the way in which the Department of Health, was able to influence the direction the group took, by fixing its parameters from the outset. In a sense, the independence of the group meant that it was caught between the demands of central government and the demands of the medical elites in the units. Independent review bodies have, of course, been in similar situations in the past, but in trying to work within a traditional rational planning framework the group found that it had to cope with the additional problem of the uncertainties that markets were now introducing.

Markets

The group focused on trying to reconcile a rational planning process with the introduction of markets. Markets were seen by some as having positive benefits, others focused on the fragmentary qualities of markets and the dangers this entailed for providing a consistent service. These concerns developed into attempts to identify ways of managing markets and controlling their negative consequences:

C3   That's a very important part of all of this set up isn't it that if they suddenly fragment the purchasers you could easily end up with black holes round the place.

M2   Well I suspect that even if there were fragmentation, there isn't any but if there were to be, I think arrangements could be made.

The clinicians were therefore prone to be more sceptical of the market, seeing it as having a destabilising potential whilst the managers were eager to dispel these fears. They were unhappy with any view of the market as having a disruptive effect and were eager to highlight that the market could be managed:

M1   I think that relates to some of the issues around trying to understand what marketing means now which isn't necessarily the cut and thrust of the street market but more the John Lewis, Marks and Spencer examples where you have a preferred provider, supplier and you do develop with that person a particular relationship. You look at venture revenue and venture capital together because that reduces your overall purchasing costs...I think that there will be a fragility in this market for a long time to come, but if we develop preferred provider models it actually allows both sides of the organisation to win something out of it.

The managers clearly saw themselves as having the role of legitimising the market. They were at pains to persuade the more sceptical clinicians on the group that a raw aggressive market was not going to be unleashed, and that they had the theoretical and practical capacity to manage the market. Such a strategy relied heavily on persuasion using rhetoric that was immersed in the technical language of quasi-markets. It is important to recognise the capacity of this technical language to form the foundations for a strategy of deception. The idea that certain models of the market can allow 'both sides to win' is clearly part of the rhetoric of markets. In addition the manager quoted above was referring to an imaginary market lying somewhere in the future, but in tones that imply that its arrival was imminent. This bore no relation to the existing conditions in London. The aim appeared to be to build a picture of a market that was controllable provided the knowledge base of the managers was adhered to. There is clearly a measure of deception at work here. Whilst open in support of the market, their approach contained elements of concealed strategic action which involved some conscious deception (in persuading the clinicians that they had the situation under control) and unconscious deception (in convincing themselves of the aims of their speech acts). Self deception comes about through the creation of a collage of terms and ideas such as 'preferred provider models', 'venture revenue' and 'market fragility' that gloss over the more immediate concerns of what the market is capable of in terms of hospital closure. Through the build up of layer upon layer of jargon, eventually the self deception is complete and can be seen in the managers attempts to establish that they had frameworks for evaluating the impact of the market on service provision and patient care:

M1   one establishes a corporate contract with Region...so there is
       an actual framework and then in fact one has to use various
       efficiency or other terminology to find a way which can
       demonstrate you've improved local health care year on year.

This is an interesting choice of words, for it suggests that what matters here is not so much the real effect of changes on service provision, but the ability to construct a language that can demonstrate improvements in health care. This aspect of the renal review group's debates raises the question as to whether managers were concerned with the ability of the market to address health care needs, or more concerned with the creation of a new technical discourse that of itself would demonstrate the beneficial effects of the market. It is here that the dangers of combining the rhetoric of need with the ideology of the market should become apparent. 'Improving health care' is not the goal in the above statement. The goal is the construction of a set of codes that are then accepted by professional groupings to signify improvements in health care. Relating this to Habermas' view that engaging in discourse assumes the validity of the discourse act, what is at stake is the extent to which the kind of discourse shown above is able to colonise the speech acts of decision makers to such an extent that it becomes impossible to distinguish between debates concerning 'real' needs and debates that are infused with an ideology that uses the discourse of needs for other purposes. For Habermas, "practical discourse is a procedure for testing the validity of hypothetical norms not for producing justified norms" (Habermas 1990, p. 122). Clearly what the manager was aiming for in the above statement is a language which is believed to produce justified norms. The reliance of the group on an epidemiological framework for discussing needs made it easier for distortions like this to operate, but it is not clear whether the existence of a framework based on a comprehensive theory of need could have prevented them from operating. In light of this it is important to explore the ways in which managers could contribute to the legitimation of distortions through the creation of a parallel technical discourse based on markets.

The issue of markets influenced the way the group members saw their role. The clinicians on the group were particularly concerned about this, and it is interesting to note that the managers on the group intervened in these discussions to try to reassure clinicians that what they were doing was worthwhile, and that the ambivalence between planning a service and the market was not a problem:

M2   Can I offer, I think, something that might make you feel a little more comfortable about that. As one of the authors of working for patients, I don't worry about that and I think the point is, or one of the points is, that we do not have a mature balanced market. Our job is first of all to put that in place instead of something unbalanced with literally twice as many centres as plainly there ought to be, so I don't think you need feel embarrassed about planning the pre-market stage of all this.

Once more the managers were engaged in giving the review group legitimacy in the face of market imperatives. The problem with renal services was not that there was too much provision, but that provision was in the wrong place and may even have been insufficient. The problem therefore was how to produce a massive restructuring of services. The contradiction was, if the market could not deliver such a structural change why was it being advocated as a solution? The chairman of the group saw such arguments as being crucial to how the group's report would be implemented:

T   I have only one reservation about that and that is where one writes the report and then goes away and if you're not careful the report goes to one side and everyone goes their own sweet way ...and I think that it's going to need a little bit more than, you know, a bag of chocolates, to pin it down you'd need a gun.

The clinicians on the group were therefore voicing concerns about the extent to which writing a rational plan could be reconciled with a market. There was no doubt in their minds that if the review group's report was to be implemented, then control mechanisms would need to be set up to keep the purchasers and providers committed to the plan. There was uncertainty as to who would ensure that such mechanisms would be set up and whether central government would want such mechanisms to exist. It was this uncertainty that affected the dynamics of the group, particularly the tensions between the interests of the doctors on the group and those of the managers. The manager (M2) described the group's role as 'planning the pre-market stage'. This implies that, provided the group set up something planned and well 'balanced', the market could be allowed to function. This can be contrasted with T's concern with the danger that the plan could be by-passed by the market once the group's work was completed. The concerns about the market seemed to instigate a search for mechanisms that would protect and enforce the recommendations of the group *in the face* of market imperatives. This highlights the way in which group debates were based around positive and negative interpretations of markets. One interpretation saw the power of markets as a locus for change and the other interpretation searched for an alternative source of power to counteract the destructive qualities of the market. The group members were therefore struggling with different understandings of markets. These differences remained unresolved throughout the group's lifetime and yet the group was able to function despite these difficulties. This reflects the capacity within the group to raise these issues without threatening a complete breakdown in communication. Individuals understood that there was no possibility of consensus nor was it likely that they could persuade others to change their opinions. In this sense there were elements of posturing in the statements of the managers and the clinicians involved. The fluidity of strategic action was an important characteristic of these debates, as actors used different types of strategic action depending on the issue being debated and their view of their relative power vis-à-vis other group members.

Protection of interests

The clinicians formed the most powerful interest on the group, managers had a particular dynamic with respect to the clinicians whilst the nurses, research staff and patient representative had much weaker roles. It is interesting however to note that the issue of nursing, particularly the poor standards of care across London led to conflicts of interest because a prestigious academic unit was singled out for criticism:

N1   At _____ for instance, which when we visited presented a
      very good report about the academic quality of the hospital
      and in fact went on about it at some length, but their nursing
      service was quite the worst I've ever seen.

The clinicians attempted to place this criticism in the context of poor nursing standards across the capital, but the unit was singled out on more than one occasion for its poor nursing standards. It was also significant that some members of the group had specific loyalties to this unit:

C1   This situation is not just confined to renal medicine. I mean I
     have had the occasion in cardiac recently to experience it, as
     someone from the inside, and there is a similar picture there
     I'm sure.
N1   I agree with you I agree with you.
T   It isn't just _____ to be fair.
N1   Oh no it's not just _____

This represented a mini crisis within the group as those who wished to see the future of this unit secured were forced to develop strategies to deflect the criticisms of the quality of services. There were considerable discussions within and outside the group to try to address this. The criticisms however could not be dismissed; in response to this the most powerful clinicians on the group began to argue that problems of service quality could be addressed but once a unit's research capacity was lost it would be 'lost forever'. Nevertheless, the nurse had clearly exposed a prestigious unit's weakness in terms of service quality. This led one clinician to resort to appealing, as 'someone from the inside', that other specialties have similar problems, suggesting that he had access to privileged information. Once the nurse conceded this, the argument that this problem was not specific to that unit was raised and an appeal to 'fairness' was made before the nurse conceded this point as well. This was clearly a strategy to deflect an argument based on evidence with arguments based on the intuitive knowledge of powerful individuals. This illustrates the sophisticated nature of the arguments employed to persuade some members of the group to conform in support of vested interests. It also reveals the nature of the forces that any attempt to place debates about need on a rational footing would have to contend with. This is as true for Doyal and Gough's rules for 'rational and democratic discussion of needs' as for any other. The capacity of such forces to remain hidden from view, forming Lukes' third face of power, even if Doyal and Gough's rules were to be followed in future debates cannot be underestimated.

Outside pressures and influences

There were considerable outside pressures on the group ranging from the Department of Health's concern to ensure that deadlines and its agenda were being adhered to, to the more wide ranging pressures of trying to plan an expansion in provision in the context of a British economy in decline:

T   you've got a country which is 50 billion in the red externally,
        20 million internal deficit and you try to increase financial
        provision for a particular group of patients who immediately
        hit the headlines every day and how do you deal with this...
        well you really have to look at the cost-effectiveness of your
        programme whether you could bring costs down even below
        your present minimum. So I think cost-effectiveness is
        crucial to the expansion which we foreshadow clearly.

This articulated the attempt by members of the group to anticipate the
repercussions of their identifying gaps in service provision. They had to
build a strategy for reconciling their highlighting 'unmet need', with the
inevitable arguments about budgetary constraints. Placing the emphasis on
cost-effectiveness was identified as one way of doing this. A major part of
the group's strategy therefore was to anticipate any critiques of its report
either from central government, purchasers, renal units or renal patient
groups. Group members were acutely aware that the independence of the
group did not mean that it was immune from the wider structural influences
affecting the NHS as a whole. Here we see the danger of focusing too
narrowly on the inter-relationships of group members, and the rationality of
internal group debates, at the expense of external factors. The ways in which
group debates could be tailored by exogenous factors are revealed, together
with the importance of situating debates within a wider social and political
context. The relationship between the balance of power within the group and
external forces was not lost on its members who linked it with the question
of accountability of the whole review process. One clinician on the group
neatly linked these issues to the question of the accountability of the market:

C9   if you now strip down to 5 units, they're going to be very
        powerful, all powerful providers and you will have to find
        some way of balancing the authority and monopoly of those
        five provider services, or they will turn around and say well
        you take it and what choice will you have. And the choice I
        offer you is that you have to find ways of getting a much
        stronger voice for patients. It's been notably absent in these
        few days the patient association not being here.

Although the review group consulted with patient groups and had a patient
association representative as a member, this consultation was restrictive and
limited in scope. Clearly the review failed to engage in open and democratic
debate with those actors most affected by its decisions. There was of course a
trade off between the degree of openness and accountability that was
possible, and the practical necessity of producing a report in a given time

scale. Members of the group were not only aware of the problems of accountability, but were also concerned that the market was capable of reinforcing this lack of accountability. They were not however, able to translate this awareness into attempts to make the review process more open. The point being made by C9 had uncomfortable implications for the group's work. Its failure to engage with patient representatives was being contrasted with the proposed creation of five very powerful centralised suppliers. This is an indication of the extent to which the membership of the group placed constraints on its discussion of health care needs and health service provision. The exclusion of patient groups, the medical dominance on the group and the gender bias of the group, all contributed towards the creation of specific parameters to the group's debates. Habermas' communicative ethics has provided the theoretical basis for exposing and analysing these exclusions and parameters. These parameters could be breached by individuals like C9 criticising the process of the review, but these criticisms could not develop sufficient momentum to deflect the review group from its main objective (be it conscious or unconscious), which was to justify the proposed model for future service provision. It is here that the group's function as an agent of legitimacy becomes most apparent.

Conclusion

This analysis suggests that the debates of the review group were not open and democratic, but were constrained firstly by the exclusion of actors affected by the group's decisions and secondly by the operation of power, both within and outside the group. This latter constraint was manifested in the strategic action of group members and individuals outside the group. The dynamics of the review process were related to the presence of markets within the NHS. The limits to the review process were not a result of health care markets, clearly previous independent reviews had suffered from similar limitations before the introduction of the market reforms. However, the existence of the market gave the review process another dimension that affected the relationship between different stakeholders. In particular, markets allowed managers to construct their own area of specialisation that had the capacity to constrain the already limited epidemiological approach to need constructed by the doctors. In the next chapter I expand my discussion to consider the implications of the findings presented in this exemplar for the development of a wider critique of NHS policy.

Notes

1   The analysis presented in this book uses a framework, based on Habermas' critical social theory and Doyal and Gough's *Theory of Human Need*, to present a historical case study of the London review of renal services both in relation to the assessment of needs made and the review group's decision making processes. This evaluation is based on an analysis of the technical information produced by the review group as an assessment of the needs of renal patients and the minutes and tapes of the renal review group's meetings. A three phase structure for a methodology of depth hermeneutics has been developed by Thompson (1981). These three stages are social analysis, discourse analysis and interpretation. They should be considered, not as discrete stages on a linear path of analysis but as thematic dimensions of an interpretative process (Pile 1990). Social analysis involves an identification and analysis of the circumstances in which people act. This incorporates historical, institutional and geographical aspects. Social analysis is undertaken at the levels of action, the institution, and structure. An analysis of action examines the context of human experience and the understandings individuals have of this context. With respect to the renal review this involved examining the review group discussions and decisions, considering the context in which these decisions were made and critically evaluating the recommendations made in the review group report. An institutional analysis recognises that institutions provide the conditions for action and the location for power relations. The source of material for this study and the field for social relations is the provision of renal services in London. The epidemiological evidence gathered by the review group to back up its recommendations was an important part of this material but in order to place this material in its historical, economic and geo-political context there was a need to supplement it with a review of national and international aspects of renal services and an understanding of how the health service market for renal services was starting to operate. This was achieved by an analysis of renal service provision in the UK and abroad. A structural analysis is introduced by looking at the parameters that defined the review group's working limits and the constraints placed on the individuals involved. This meant the study of technical data used by the review group, their perceptions of it and an analysis of the groups communicative understanding of the needs assessment process. The task of discourse analysis is to examine meanings with the aim of getting deeper understandings of the way discourse sustains power relations. Discourse analysis is undertaken at levels of narrative, argumentative

114

structure and syntactic structure. An analysis of narratives looks at the use of myths, stories and anecdotes in justifying existing power relations. Argumentative structures are forms of discourse made up of explanations and 'chains of reasoning'. By reconstructing these 'chains of reasoning' it may be possible to expose contradictions and inconsistencies in arguments. Finally by the analysis of syntactic structure (the use of pronouns, structure of tenses etc.) we can see the way processes are represented as things outside of immediate time and space and can therefore be discussed at 'arms length'. In this way it may be possible to gain insights into how ideology exists within linguistic forms. Finally, interpretation is a fusion of social analysis and discourse analysis into a comprehensive account of the 'lifeworld'. Interpretation goes beyond analysis by projecting possible meanings on the discourse. This is not an attempt to confirm a single identifiable reality but an exploration of the different foundations for the actions of stakeholders and in this sense considers the 'situated work' of the stakeholders (Silverman 1985). By weaving together social and discourse analysis into an interpretation of actions the analysis makes a claim to 'truth' whilst acknowledging that it is still only an interpretation. By participating in the production and reproduction of the lifeworld (in this case the lifeworld of policy makers) the analysis presented here attempts to develop an interpretation that combines hermeneutic understanding and causal explanation. The technical data on needs used in the needs assessment process is related to Doyal and Gough's theory of need. The Focus is on the way in which an epidemiological definition of need was chosen and documented by the group together with the group's proposed plan for future services. This is then situated within a historical, geographical and economic analysis of renal services provision in the UK and abroad. This forms the basis for social analysis using a framework where a comparison is made between the review groups use and understanding of traditional needs assessment: epidemiology, survival data, outcome data, cost data and travel times with the framework for operationalising needs demanded by Doyal and Gough's theory of needs. The official record of the review is contrasted with the discourses contained in the taped recordings of group discussions to develop a deeper understanding of the way needs were interpreted and used in the policy process. To facilitate this the analysis is structured by dividing the actors involved into groups; managers, academics and medics, using Alford's (1975) interest groups and Mitroff's (1983) stakeholders as models.

115

2   Transcription symbols:

( )	untranscribable passage
(conflict)`	unclear utterance
(0.5)	silence in seconds
(...)	passage not transcribed
...	passage not included in quote
_____ or [W]	Name deleted to preserve anonymity

These markers appear before each passage of transcript as a guide to its origin.

T	Chair of group
M1,2...	Manager
C1,2...	Clinician
A1,2...	Academic
N1,2...	Nurse

6 Needs and the political economy of the health service

This book has examined theories of need and justice with respect to health policy. The importance of power and the systemised nature of health care decision making has been highlighted using an analysis of the planning of provision of renal services in the South East of England as an exemplar. The analysis has focused on the definitions of needs used, the rationale for decision making and the repercussions for purchasing services in the reformed NHS. This exemplar was chosen because the dilemmas in health policy that arise in this area of health care, where needs are acute and resources are rationed, bring questions of justice to the surface. It is clear from the previous chapters that there are vulnerable groups within populations whose need for, and use of, services varies and their relationship with the system is uncertain. At the time of the renal review the system was experiencing continuous structural change and financial stringency. Within these parameters managers and clinicians alike had to make hard decisions concerning prioritisation of resources. Many commentators at the time looked at how these decisions were made implicitly, to what extent they should become more explicit and how this could best be achieved. This book has considered a theoretical basis for such decision making and looked at how decisions were arrived at in practice.

To summarise the discussion thus far I have considered the relevance of alternative notions of need to health policy and emphasised the importance of the principle of justice in the search for a defensible health policy. Doyal and Gough (1991) refer to the harm that occurs when needs are not met as disabled social participation. Intermediate needs such as health care should therefore be organised on the basis of the goal of minimising disabled social participation. If health policy is to be based on such a theory of need then the objective of minimising disabled social participation will require a framework for reaching consensus and agreement on definitions of disability and autonomy, measures of disability and autonomy and the processes by which measurement is undertaken. Their theory can therefore be split into a substantive part which identifies basic needs, and a procedural part which provides a framework for resolving disputes concerning policies for achieving a goal of need satisfaction (Gough and Thomas 1994). In Chapter 3 I explored the potential a communicative ethics holds for producing a framework for discussing these issues. Theories of power in the NHS were related to the development of quasi-markets in health care and I considered the role of health care needs in this development. Finally, the possibilities that Habermas' work held for evaluating assessments of health care needs were considered, both in terms of the way needs are identified and the way needs are debated and agreed upon.

Using the independent review of renal services in London as an exemplar I considered the work of the review in relation to Doyal and Gough's rules for discussing needs and Habermas' communicative ethics. In chapter 4, I discussed the technical limitations of the review process, the constrained definitions of need used, and placed the review group's decisions in the social, economic and geo-political context of a service that has been historically underfunded. Gaps in the review group's technical knowledge of needs were identified along with the possible effects this had on the 'rationality' of decision making. In chapter 5, I considered the review process from a participatory viewpoint and the minutes of review group meetings, and the transcribed tapes of meetings were analysed. Using Habermas' communicative ethics as a basis for this analysis it was possible to highlight the ways in which vested interests were able to operate to distort the understandings of need, and how different definitions of need were used as part of the strategic actions of powerful groups. Not only were these ideological distortions able to operate in the gaps left by a lack of technical knowledge of need, but also they contributed to maintaining a particular and restricted view of needs that set constraints on the search for technical knowledge. This analysis suggested that the renal review was part of a process of managing the rationalisation of service in London and the simultaneous managing of the newly developing quasi-market in health care. Within this process appeals to need had a positive aspect in that they were used to challenge existing inequity and to challenge the potential inequities arising form the changes to the system. Simultaneously appeals to need had a negative aspect in their capacity to reinforce the claims of vested interests. This analysis can also be applied to the presence of quasi-markets in that needs could challenge markets or legitimise them depending on circumstances and the way needs were defined. The drive towards markets and greater competition within the health care sector failed to take account of the need for a framework for discussing needs. On the contrary they made the possibility of such a framework more remote.

Some of the gaps between decision making in theory and in practice have been highlighted and the extent to which these gaps were filled with the ideology of powerful interest groups has been explored. If these problems are to be addressed in the future then this analysis implies that health policy should contain a commitment to a normative domain of procedural guidelines for discussing needs. This final chapter considers the contradictions involved in a welfare system whose aim is to ensure that there is universal access to basic human needs whilst at the same time operating as part of the modern capitalist state.

Implications for interpreting UK health policy

Since the work of the Resource Allocation Working Party (RAWP 1976), the UK has been moving towards addressing the issue of equity in health care, but it is questionable whether this movement has been based on a clear theory of need. The move towards quasi-markets within a system where resources are allocated firstly on the basis of capitation and then on the basis of contracts added a further dimension to the problem. This case study of renal services has shown that inequalities in health care provision exist and that these are diverse in origin and are based on the dimensions of geography, race, culture, gender, class and socio-economic status. It is questionable whether a model based on the centralised allocation of funds, within which competitive markets were encouraged to operate, could provide the necessary conditions to address such inequality. What is more clear is that different understandings of need exist at various levels in the system. This is particularly true of understandings of the levels of need to be met by the provision of welfare and the levels of need ascribed to individuals. This presents problems for any attempt to assess the gap between the objectives of the system and the extent to which the system was meeting needs. The analysis presented in this book shows how the rhetoric of need can be employed by vested interests. This suggests that the fundamental ideal of a service based on the principles of justice and need can be compromised by the injection of procedures that allow prejudice to operate, albeit covertly or unintentionally. This has important consequences for the problems raised by a health system experiencing continuous change. Its structures and processes cannot escape the questions of how, and by whom, individuals are to be valued. This phenomenon, and the way actors at a level removed from central government adapt changes to the system to their own view of the system, is an important area for the study of policy and its effects on needs. On a policy level, what is interesting is the extent to which the problems identified by the work presented in this book operated despite policy objectives, or because of the faultlines of policy itself.

It is useful to consider the relationship between framework (the extent to which the health care system is fixed or open to change) and compliance (the extent to which the framework complies with the fundamental principles of social justice and need satisfaction), (Curtis 1989). This facilitates a policy analysis based on whether the structure of the health care system contains inequalities and injustices and the relationship of these structural problems to sub-structures within the institution. The analysis can also be enriched by the understanding that the dynamics of health policy is based on power relationships, but that the key to these relationships is the inter-dependencies within structural constraints (Harrison et al 1990). In this sense structures have a different and wider meaning, so that structural constraints are the increasing elderly population, decreasing economic growth, past legacies such as ageing hospitals and labour market constraints such as nursing shortages. The arguments presented in this book have drawn on the idea that policy making, within these constraints, is not governed by 'rational planning' but is the product of a bargaining process between interdependent power relationships; 'a network or bargaining community' (Harrison et al 1990). This implies that health care decision-making is not underpinned by a theory of need and justice, but is determined by a bargaining process. The impact that quasi-markets had on this bargaining process cannot be underestimated. This process was strongly situated in the language of need making it difficult to distinguish between 'genuine' appeals to need and the use of 'needs' to support vested interests. Often patient needs and vested interests overlapped making the process more complex and difficult to interpret. This can be seen in the way in which the medics on the review group were able to use evidence of 'unmet need' to argue for more resources, improvements in services as well as justify decisions that protected vested interests.

It is possible to consider contracting between purchasers and providers as the bargaining process formalised at a micro level. Indeed, supporters of the market argued that it had the potential to do exactly this because contracts made decision making more explicit and decision makers more accountable. This 'explicit' characteristic of quasi-markets, it was argued, gave the rationing debate a new importance (Heginbotham et al 1992). In the past the process of priority setting had been a political one. Policies were set at a national level and moulded at a local level by professional interests. Heginbotham et al argued that the purchaser-provider split had the potential to challenge 'provider capture'; that is, the ability of powerful provider interests to direct where resources were to be allocated. By creating separate purchasing organisations the reforms gave purchasers responsibility to look at local needs, local morbidity patterns and consumers' views and allocate resources accordingly. Purchasers also had a responsibility to examine the cost-effectiveness of services. Although it is important to recognise that there were strong elements of technocratic decision making in this process it is clear that there was potential here for altering the balance of power between professional groups. Whereas rationing in the NHS has always been an implicit process that sometimes explodes into the public domain by means of headline cases such as children not receiving high technology care or 'tramps' being refused renal treatment, the reforms had the potential to put rationing on a different level. This is an important point, but it should be tempered by the possibility that quasi-markets could also operate as a mechanism for reducing accountability, concealing decision making and stifling debate. Whilst quasi-markets possessed this duality the policy process was not grounded in a theory of need based on a communicative ethics. Very often contracts and planning documents had a specialised language that provided a 'linguistic smoke screen' for undemocratic processes. The renal review debates showed how managers used the existence of markets, and their presumed knowledge of health care markets, to discourage open decision making and to limit debates on need and justice. The 'fairness' of market solutions were not in doubt, provided the managers were allowed the role of 'managing markets'. In a sense managers and the 'market' based discourses they developed acted as a 'glue' that maintained the process of change and gave the changes legitimacy.

It is important to situate this discussion of health care needs within the limits of health care policies and resource constraints at the time. There is some 'rationing frontier' beyond which resources cannot be allocated without denying care to moral equals. The inevitability of rationing was linked to arguments concerning the increasing elderly population and the widening gap between what was technically possible and what resources allowed. Some based these arguments on a model of exponential growth of public/professional expectations and resources, with expectations outstripping the capacity of resources to meet them (Thwaites 1987). Indeed Thwaites argued that his simple model:

> explains, on the one hand, governmental exasperation that
> the ever increasing funding of the NHS goes unappreciated;
> and on the other, the readiness of the medical profession and
> the public to believe that the NHS is being increasingly
> severely cut. (p. 17)

Arguments that draw on concepts such as infinite demands and the growing elderly population have the potential to create a moral panic that justifies attacks on the welfare system. It is important therefore to situate arguments within this context if policy responses to the gap between resources, technology and expectations are to be understood. In this sense Thwaites' analysis was incomplete. The essential question with respect to quasi-markets in health care was: what was being managed? Was it *need* or was it *expectations* that the market was dealing with? This question went to the heart of the renal review group's debates. The medical professionals on the group interpreted need at two levels: the numbers of potential patients in a population and access to services. The managers on the group did not challenge the medical definition of need but they directed the group's debates towards a limited and restricted understanding of access to services, arguing that the proper place for determining access was the market. In this way they seemed to be attempting to assert their domain of influence over accounts of the gap between need, resources and expectations. The focus of rationing seemed to be directed through the policy process towards dealing with expectations rather than needs. The implication of this for interpreting UK health policy is that the market may have been presented as an attempt to allocate resources in a rational manner, but manifested itself by impinging on the system as an exercise in legitimacy.

The relationship between need and legitimation has formed a pivotal part of this book. Salter (1993, 1998) points out that the popular perception of a universal NHS, free at the point of use, places no ideological barriers on individual demands for health. In these circumstances, where resources are limited by capitation, there will always be a mismatch between consumer demand and demand defined by purchasers. The reconciliation of these two forces requires, in part, a selling of purchasing decisions to the public. In other words, purchasers have to ensure legitimacy in the eyes of their local populations. The process of legitimisation could focus on purchasing itself, or on addressing expectations, but as Salter argues:

> Once it is recognised that explicit rationing and the expectations created by the NHS myth are mutually incompatible, and that the gap between the two cannot be bridged simply by characterising the purchasing process as democratic and rational, other political forms have to be found to resolve the conundrum. The choice is between changing the expectations and changing the purchasing process. To date, the focus has been upon the latter. (Salter 1993, p. 179)

Rationing and rationalisation in the NHS

Rationing services by 'rational' means has become a central part of health policy debates. Resource scarcity and finite funding arrangements are seen as axiomatic for politicians, policy makers, managers and professionals alike. These developments received an impetus from the shifts towards quasi-markets and a culture of discipline and parsimony in resource use which can be caricatured in terms of replacing high trust relations with low trust relations. Such systemisation (based on mechanistic rational solutions) is attractive to politicians and policy makers who are seeking solutions to the spiralling cost of health care. Hard political choices are transformed into technical solutions and policy is thereby depoliticised. The disciplining nature of the corporate, technocratic state is reinforced by reference to the 'given' 'natural' state of rationing. But where political discourse is displaced by the language of prioritisation (buttressed by technically defined 'needs') a possible sub-text is the delegitimisation of efforts to incorporate meaning, culture, history and values into the debate. The 'needs' based solutions offered by professionals are based in knowledge, rather than in people. In contrast to the rationality of the system world, lay knowledge is experiential and all too easily dismissed as 'non-scientific'. However, lay knowledge is rooted in the material reality of people's lives. That it is to say it is based on experiences people have in material circumstances. The epistemological foundations of people's everyday knowledge means that claims for the 'objectivity' of expert knowledge are contestable. Lay knowledge offers political challenges to the apparent role of professionals in determining the way in which questions are framed, problems are defined and knowledge is used in the policy arena (Williams and Popay 1994). The exemplar of renal services shows how easily these tendencies can be taken for granted and accepted as the natural order of things. In light of this, we should be wary of calls for public debates of rationing that are prefaced by conditions that can force these contested spaces into parameters defined by the inevitability of rationing and professionally defined 'need' all of which tend to delegitimate public opposition.

Rationing and Rationalisation therefore are inextricably linked. Just as 'rationing' is characterised by inevitability, it is, in turn, inevitably tied to the consequences of rationalisation. To ignore these consequences is to loose sight of the ways in which modern organisational bureaucracies place everyday lives within technocratic frameworks.

Rationing is perceived and portrayed in different settings by health professionals, by politicians and the media. It is interesting therefore to consider for a while the ways in which rationing is increasingly 'depoliticised' in different ways within these different arenas.

Health professionals

Talk of rationing has filled the pages of the medical press throughout the 1990s with leaders of the medical and managerial professions becoming increasingly frustrated with politician silence on this issue. In a BMJ editorial of 22nd June 1996 Richard Smith wrote:

In Britain neither the government nor the main opposition party will openly acknowledge the inevitability of rationing health care. Instead, they talk of increasing the effectiveness of health care, spending more on the health service, and setting priorities locally.

He went on to make a clear separation between issues of effectiveness, underfunding and rationing arguing that:

The debate over rationing should not be confused with debates over effectiveness and funding of the health service. Few people disagree with the need to increase effectiveness, and there is little controversy about denying ineffective treatment. Many people in the health service think that more funds should be available for health care, and many members of the public support such a proposal. But these are separate debates. More effectiveness and more money will not remove the need to deny effective treatments.

The distinction between technical issues of effective treatment, political issues of global funding and rationing are made abundantly clear. For this commentator (and for many others) it would appear that 'rationing' occupies a separate space that has its own unquestionable logic. Rationing is inevitable, and unavoidable. Nevertheless, it would appear that political engagement is required for he concluded:

Britain's next government must take a lead on health care rationing. (Smith 1996)

More recently the debate has moved forward to focus not on whether rationing in health care is acceptable but on whether rationing should be *implicit* or *explicit* (Maxwell 1995, Doyal 1997, Coast 1997).

Acceptance of the 'inevitability' of rationing and frustration with political inertia is not confined to the medical press and academic debate. In 1996 the Director of Public Health for East London launched her annual report that had effective health care as its theme, with the statement:

All of us - patients, doctors and health authorities - want effective health care. In practice this means that all of us - indeed society as a whole - need to accept that rationing which reduces ineffective care and releases money to be spent on effective health care will benefit health. (Jacobson 1996)

These views were expanded upon in the main body of the report:

> It is an inescapable truth that there is never sufficient money to meet all needs and wants. It is therefore, naive to oppose all forms of rationing. Whilst politicians might argue that rationing does not occur, it has always occurred and always will. Our challenge is to ration explicitly and fairly. This should be done by rationing, as far as is possible, on the basis of evidence of effectiveness and cost effectiveness. This does not mean that services should be 'stopped' or 'cut' overnight. There is rarely sufficient evidence to do this. More importantly, we have to recognise that we are not building and planning services from scratch. We have to recognise patterns of care that have built up over many years and change is probably best achieved 'at the margin' bit by bit. This means that we should not abandon all tonsillectomies, but should define more strictly who is most likely to benefit.

Such sentiments can be found in health authorities and trusts across the country. The increasing vocalisation of 'rationing' as an issue in the NHS can be seen in the formation of the Rationing Agenda Group (RAG) which was set up to "...deepen the British debate on rationing health care." On the basis that:

> rationing health care is inevitable and that the public must be involved in the debate about issues relating to rationing. (New B 1996)

This group was formed from a disparate band of members including ethicists, health authority members, GPs, Health Economists, Academics, Researchers and Journalists, with clearly differing views but a common aim of setting:

> an agenda of all the issues that need to be considered when debating the rationing of health care.

In doing this they claimed that they:

> present as neutrally as possible all the issues related to rationing and priority setting in the NHS...though our position is neutral, we hold two substantive views - namely, that rationing is unavoidable and that there should be more explicit debate about the principles and issues concerned.

125

There are differences in emphasis among all three examples but the logic of rationing is a common theme to all. In parallel with this lies the desire to expose the issue of rationing to political and public debate and to place political and public debates within the logical boundaries of 'rationing'.

It should not be forgotten that these arguments and developments have taken place when health care systems are experiencing considerable pressures as a result of structural changes in health care. Such changes make it difficult to clearly demarcate the boundaries between global resourcing, effectiveness and rationing. Perhaps because of this the reluctance of politicians to give rationing a formal status is a phenomenon that transcends political boundaries.

Politicians

As we have seen, during the 1980s the Conservative government's strategy to introduce management and competition into the financing and delivery of the National Health Service (NHS) reflected the success of the New Right in arguing against collective methods of financing and for a greater emphasis on individual responsibility. Calls for more choice were married to concerns about increasing health care costs and the size of public sector borrowing. This ideology allowed public services to be subjected to the disciplining force of resource constraints whilst by-passing the problem of 'rationing' with arguments that emphasised the right of individuals to go outside the public sector to buy services.

Despite attacking public services as wasteful and over bureaucratised and despite introducing market reforms the conservative government maintained a preference for continuing with the invisible, implicit and diffuse form of rationing that has characterised the British NHS. In the words of one Conservative Secretary of State for Health:

> Our approach is partly a bottom up approach, that health authorities working with local people, and above all working with local GPs, need to educate, inform, have a dialogue about what is achievable and what is the best way of setting priorities in a particular community. (Quoted in Hunter 1995 p. 880)

On the left rationing was taken up as an issue by think tanks such as the PSI (PSI 1993) but the Labour party clearly avoided using the term in its policy document Health 2000 preferring instead to state that:

> Governments world-wide have been examining ways in which satisfactory control can be exercised on the upward pressure on health spending...

126

The document proposed the establishment of a panel made up of professionals and patient representatives to:

> develop national guidelines for the allocation of scarce resources. Advice might also be offered where difficult or ethical judgements have to be made.(Labour Party 1994, p. 82)

More recently in its white paper (DoH 1997) the Labour government rejected arguments that the NHS is unable to accommodate resource pressures preferring to state:

> Nor are the arguments in favour of rationing or charging convincing.

Instead the white paper proposes a 'third way' of running the NHS. Clearly there is an acceptance of having to address the consequences of bureaucratic structures facing finite resources but there is an equal and common desire to avoid the explicit recognition of rationing as a political fact.[1]

The media

Freemantle and Harrison (1993) show how rationing has been dealt with by the media. Taking Baudrillard's lead they identify a tendency among the popular press to present simplistic and one dimensional views of rationing dilemmas, personalising what are profound social issues by offering mythical versions of events. In contrast they identified coverage in so called quality papers as technocratic introducing an alternative mythology based on depersonalising rationing dilemmas. In the creation of both mythological forms the political nature of rationing is avoided.

It would appear therefore that health professionals, politicians and the media address rationing in different ways but all have a common tendency to 'depoliticise' what is essentially a political question.

Lay participation, rationing and the 'new' NHS

The extent and depth of lay participation in health care decision making varies tremendously. This is so despite the WHO stating that lay involvement in health care decision making is a social, economic and technical necessity (Waterworth and Luker 1990) and despite the considerable energy that has been spent in recent years on developing innovative and productive strategies for user involvement (Kelson 1995, 1997). The NHS has made public participation a priority (DoH 1996, 1997) making a strong distinction between the involvement of people at the level of individual treatment and care and the level of service development (the level of citizens and communities). Evidence to show the most effective ways of enhancing patient choice and patient participation is in very short supply (Calnan, Halik and Sabbat 1998). The limited number of research studies in this field suggest that patients want to be involved in decision making but as yet little is known about the ways in which they can become more involved and even less is known about the benefits of their involvement (Guadagnoli and Ward 1998).

In contrast there is a wide array of literature on priority setting within health care (Klein et al 1996, New and Le Grand 1996). Theoretical models of equitable resource allocation have been developed and critically compared and empirical research into the degree and cause of scarcity within the NHS has been completed.

Participation in health care decision has not been adequately evaluated (Charles and DeMaio 1993) but it is useful to distinguish between public and private participation. *Private* participation refers to the involvement of individuals in their own care and treatment. The benefits of participation at this level according to McEwen et al (1983) include; increasing patient involvement; more commitment to health and health-promoting behaviours; the development of an ecological concept of health and improved use of health services. The risks of participation according to Brearley (1990) include possible delay in seeking care, risks of conflicting advice, misuse of technical information and alienation of professionals. *Public* participation refers to involvement in decision-making processes concerning service planning and delivery, service evaluations and consultations over future service provision. It refers to a democratisation of decision making with the public assuming greater responsibility for decisions regarding the wider aspects of health and social policy. Participation can take place at a number of levels. These have been operationalised by Arnstein (1969) in her 'ladder of citizen participation' graduating in eight stages from non-participation to citizen control. The benefits of public participation depend crucially on the pattern of re-distribution of power. The dangers and risks are that consultation becomes the norm and in the name of participation this is little more than 'window dressing' (Biehal 1993). Indeed recent research on the impact of the Conservative governments NHS reforms emphasises the unevenness of the choices available to the public and the dangers of 'tokenism' in participatory strategies (Forde-Roberts 1998).

Rationing and a 'primary care led' NHS

The increasing impetus for a primary care led NHS can be seen in the governments legislation (DoH 1997) and in the possible variety of new arrangements for organising and delivering primary care (Coulter and Mays

1997). The NHS in England is moving towards a structure based around 500 primary care groupings of some 50 GPs covering 'natural' communities of some 100,000 people. They will hold the budgets for purchasing hospital and community health services and the cash limited part of GMS funding. The government anticipates primary care groups with varying degrees of purchasing capacity. Decisions on purchasing will have important repercussions as all purchasing models involve GPs having to face dilemmas in the allocation of limited NHS resources. In particular, the need to decide what treatment to prescribe individual patients and what purchasing advice should be given to health authorities. In such circumstances ethical dilemmas are potentially magnified for the physician. This manifests itself in the USA as the courtship of the paying patient (Braithwaite 1993). There may be conflicts between the economic interest of the physician and the trustworthiness of the profession and new arrangements could have the perverse effect of increasing inequalities in access to health care (Iliffe and Munro 1993) They could also involve excessive transaction costs, perverse incentives and could frustrate attempts to plan services rationally and consistently.

Criticisms of government policies have raised the spectre of destabilisation in primary care services, particularly in inner city areas (Heath 1997). At present good research evidence of the extent and nature of conflicts and dilemmas is lacking. Equally the potential ethical benefits of different forms of primary care organisations have not been fully explored. It is clear that "primary care groups will face difficult and demanding decisions if they are to meet the objectives of the white paper on issues of quality and equity" (Butler and Rowland 1998). Indeed Bevan (1998) has argued that the 1997 white paper's implicit goals of clinical equity and financial equity are incompatible. At the same time evidence of inequalities in health care is growing and has been linked to varying access to particular drugs treatments including interferon in multiple sclerosis, statins in primary prevention of heart disease and donezepil in Alzheimer's disease (Horton 1998). The problem of rationing remains despite government claims to the contrary.

Technocratic 'solutions' to the problem of rationing

Technocratic solutions to the problems of rationing offer ways of improving decision making and offer to de-politicise the rationing debate. Health Economists for example have successfully argued for the application of the concept of opportunity cost to the problem of scarce health care resources. In basic terms Economic rationality works on the premise of maximising the utility gained from the input of a certain quantity of resources Williams (1985);

goods will be produced or resources spent up to the point were marginal benefits/utility are equal to marginal costs. Economists argue that opportunity costs are an essential part of the rational decision making process. Such processes however have to draw on reliable and accurate information on the relative effectiveness of treatments and their comparative costs and benefits. This has underpinned the movement towards Evidence Based Health Care (EBHC) a burgeoning form of technical knowledge.

This movement represents important developments and, in light of evidence suggesting significant levels of 'inappropriate' if not harmful health care (Roos et al 1990), it is to be welcomed. But as advocates of EBHC themselves have recognised (Chalmers 1995), EBHC cannot offer *certainties*. Criticised for encouraging cookbook medicine (the slavish following of guidelines) (Lancet 1995), the generalisability of EBHC has also been questioned as has its over reliance on quantitative methods at the expense of qualitative insights. In effect, the emphasis on problem solving within the context of RCTs and meta-analyses can mean that EBHC is restricted in its focus. It could also act against patient and user involvement. The manner in which interventions are taken up in practice is also important. It is here that the apparent certainties that technocratic solutions produce are subjected to the 'uncertainties' associated with processes of persuasion, decision making, implementation and confirmation. The danger lies in the elevation of these technocratic solutions by policy makers who see it as a way of getting quick solutions, legitimising difficult decisions and most importantly as a way out of the rationing debate. Hard political choices are transformed into technical solutions through focusing on mechanistic rational forms of health services research, thus imposing a rational scientific framework on what in reality is more complex, contested and ambivalent. The danger is that the system world (Habermas 1990) is reinforced through a spurious rationality embedded in biomedical positivism and the neo-classical bias of health economics. In this context the meaning of illness tends to be ignored and patients are treated as technical subjects. The belief that 'reality' consists of phenomena that can be quantified and measured is reinforced. Political discourse is displaced by the language of technique and efficiency (Jones 1995a). The paradox of these trends is that in freeing medicine from irrational and harmful effects of arbitrary practices they simultaneously act as scientific straight jackets binding health policy to narrow reductionist approaches. The attraction is one of technocratic solutions to profound policy and ethical decisions to avoid political debate.

Rationing models

Rationing takes place covertly or explicitly in all health care systems. In private systems such as the USA, rationing is done on the basis of price. In insurance based systems rationing occurs through additional costs or restricted coverage.

In the tax based system of the NHS rationing occurs through the gatekeeper role of the General Practitioner and through waiting lists (Frankel and West 1993). Waiting lists can be perceived as an efficiency device or as a sign of inefficiency, they are not necessarily a bad thing and used effectively can have beneficial results in that they allow patient admissions to be better planned and can be used to optimise the use of resources (Yates 1995). The criteria governing admission on to waiting lists as well as priority within a waiting list seems too easily manipulated by those in power. What is lacking is open debate about how waiting lists are managed and how and whether it is possible to ration within waiting lists and/or between waiting lists.

Rationing in the American Health Care system takes the form of sections of the population having a prescribed form of health coverage or being excluded from health care coverage altogether. In Oregon, quality of life scales were linked with public consultation on what treatment and condition pairs might be funded. Oregon was presented as an attempt to combine a 'rational' basis for decision making with public participation (Fox and Leichter 1991, Klein 1991). Oregon was welcomed as a 'scientific' 'technical' solution to the problem of scarcity. It compelled politicians, health care providers and the communities they serve to address rationing dilemmas 'in public' but problems of scarcity, equity and need could only be addressed within a 'rational' utilitarian framework. Critics of the Oregon approach argued that it was flawed because it used individuals as foci for measurement while largely ignoring the moral agency of human beings (Relman 1990, Hadorn 1991, Charney et al 1989). Most disturbing of all was that it targeted the poor on Medicaid whilst allowing the middle classes a primary say in how this was done. The result being that poor women and children were subjected to the rationing process but that the consultation exercise with the local community was organised in a way that gave disproportionate voice to the middle classes in the decision making process (Daniels 1991). Oregon could not escape the charge of professional elites consulting with the middle classes to introduce a public 'values system' for rationing services to the poor.

In the Netherlands, attempts to formalise health care rationing have been based on the recommendations of the Dunning Committee report of 1992 (Netherlands 1992) that included a framework for decision making that required services to pass the test of community necessity, effectiveness, efficiency and individual responsibility before being included as part of the basic package of health services. In New Zealand in 1992 a government established committee began the work of developing clinical guidelines to determine access to care. Whilst in Sweden a government committee set up in 1993 developed principles to guide decision making. These principles included human dignity, need and efficiency. Regional committees took this work forward to determine priorities in local areas. These different approaches reflect national differences in cultural understandings and differences in the comprehensiveness and form of health services. Differences that persist despite what has been termed a convergence in the structure of health service provision towards market type models (Ham and Honigsbaum 1998). However, these models share a common feature namely proscribed public involvement. That is to say public participation is restricted and problematic. Consequently:

> The risk is that those who participate in debates on priority setting have a vested interest in the outcome and articulate values that may not reflect those of the community as a whole (Ham 1995, p. 829)

"Rationality" in relation to health care

The idea that human subjectivity is compromised by rationalised systems and the accompanying processes of rationalisation that characterise modernity is not new. Weber (1978) wrote extensively about the growing influence of technological and scientific thought over different areas of social life. Traditional social organisation and traditional values became overwhelmed by the irresistible march of industrialisation resulting in human action being held fast in the 'iron cage' of purposive rationality (Giddens 1971). This analysis has been interpreted as pessimistic and fatalistic (Turner 1993) but its importance for other schools of thought cannot be underestimated (Turner 1996; Lowy 1979). This analysis also had a profound influence over Habermas' approach to rationalisation with Habermas reacting to Weber's pessimism by arguing that he was wrong in ascribing primacy to the Rationalization of structures of power over culture and ethics.

Habermas tries to free himself of the fatalism and pessimism of the 'iron cage' by arguing that ethics and culture are equally involved in the development of rationalised society. The rationalisation of ethics and culture sets limits to what can and cannot be regarded as legitimate and this acts as a break on power. However, Habermas suggests that rationality can itself be a form of domination of social relations as purposive-rational action follows the dictates of power and becomes an exercise in control rather than a product of common values. What then occurs is the replacement of the beneficial aspects of Rationalization with those that lead to domination. The late 20th century has witnessed a move away from the 'art' of administration (as envisaged by Weber) to a new scientific stage of bureaucratisation. Habermas outlines three models of bureaucratisation: *the technocratic model* (where the politician is now dependent on and an agent of a scientific intelligencia); *the expanded decisionistic model* (where new technocrats camouflage what is as political as ever) and *the pragmatic model* (involving critical interaction between expert and politician in a loop of communicative practice). Instead of Weber's distinction between the expert (working in technical and scientific spaces) and the 'politician (working in space characterised by the operation of power and the will), in the new *scientific stage* this division becomes blurred. It is no longer clear (if it ever was) who is pulling the strings. This book has suggested that these tendencies are discernible in NHS policy making and in strategic decision making of NHS professionals and managers. Scientisation permeates the health service arena with the increasing emphasis given to evidence based medicine, hierarchies of research evidence and research methods and the imperatives of health economics, echoing Habermas' earlier concerns that:

> The scientization of politics is not yet a reality, but it is a real tendency for which there is evidence. (Habermas 1989, p. 62)

Although Habermas does not accept that there is a necessary triumph of bureaucratic Rationalisation. The co-development of ethical Rationalisation also means other issues such as values and democracy also have to be addressed. He sees democracy and technocratic administration as incompatible and seems to suggest that there is a 'soiling' of the public sphere resulting in a sort of 'exhibition' of redundant values.

> The politicisation of the mass of the population and the decline of the public realm as a political institution are components of a system of domination that tends to exclude practical questions from public discussion. The bureaucratised exercise of power has its counterpart in a public realm confined to spectacles and acclamation.(Habermas 1989, p. 75)

It should be no surprise therefore that the debate regarding rationing is one where experts bemoan the public's susceptibility to 'shroud waving', parochialism and sectionalism and construct increasingly abstract ways of making priority setting as 'value-free' as possible. That the public might not accept such constructs is barely considered.

As this book suggests, it is possible to use Habermas' distinction between 'purposive rational action' and 'communicative action' to understand these trends. Health care rationing could be seen as the cutting edge of a process of 'lifeworld' colonisation by a rationality that distorts the values of the mass of the population in the interests of powerful groups. Scambler (1987) provides examples of the colonisation of the lifeworld by medicine and such colonisation has occurred through the social respect attributed to medical expertise, its social legitimation, and its formal knowledge (Friedson 1986). This is not to say that such colonisation only has one dimension. Medicine has made hugely beneficial and positive contributions to meeting generalisable needs and interests. At the same time however, its negative aspects are to be found in the inappropriate use of formal medical knowledge to justify or legitimate the vested interests of the powerful.

The NHS and welfare capitalism

In bringing the discussion of 'needs' and rationing together in this final chapter I am conscious of the consequences for Marxist approaches to the NHS (and the welfare state in general). The duality of the welfare state for Marxism is that it can be heralded as a prize for the working class (Navarro 1978, Gough 1979), but at the same time it fulfils important functions for the capitalist state (O'Connor 1973). However, the state does not act as a single entity, with the knowledge and awareness to be able to plan for the needs of capitalism. Rather it is made up of a plurality of institutions whose goals are diverse (Offe 1984). The main factors governing social policy therefore are the internal concerns of the state apparatus rather than the needs of class interests. Within this Marxist paradigm, as expectations increase, as technology changes, resources remain static and other structural considerations impinge on the state of welfare, then clearly arguments about a crisis of legitimacy come to the fore. The gap between expectations and resources is met by a plurality of policies from rational planning, decentralisation of responsibility, privatisation, contracting out and the scientisation of demands (Fitzpatrick 1987). These strategies can be clearly seen in the constraints placed on health policy by changes in the system. The scientization of demands is particularly important because it encapsulates the capacity of medical ideology to act in ways that translate health care needs into scientific issues, thus erecting a barrier between the health needs of society and the needs of the state. In this way the profession of medicine can be perceived as having an oppressive influence. Medicine becomes a medium by which the 'systemworld' colonises the 'lifeworld'. Such a view must be tempered by the insight that the medicalisation of needs still has the potential to present the state apparatus with challenges to the existing order. Recognising the fluidity of the relationship between the lifeworld and systemworld helps to explain the medical profession's role as a vehicle in a two way street. This occurs in the context of a state that is experiencing major changes in welfare provision. These changes are influenced by our understandings of 'needs', how they are defined and by whom they are defined. The state's role in allowing dominant interests the power to control areas like 'needs assessment' set the parameters for this process. This places limits on the capacity of needs to challenge existing structures and indeed contributes to the moulding of needs into forms that support vested interests. In the case of the renal review this was reinforced by the push to situate this process within a framework of quasi-markets. 'Needs' were dressed in the language of 'choice' and 'consumer rights', and were seen as 'liberating' the individual from a bureaucratic system. These were the emperors new clothes however, for 'needs' were captured by the demands of the systemworld. Their enabling potential was dwarfed by the part they played in the system's means of surveillance and social control. This case study of renal services has shown how a medicalised definition of need can challenge inequalities and force a response from within the system. However, the limits of this medicalised definition have also been exposed in that ultimately it was tied to the interests of medical elites. This suggests that challenges to inequalities of health, based on the medicalisation of needs, are constrained by the medical framework within which they are formed. It is through this kind of analysis that it becomes possible to argue that while the capitalist system exists through the commodification of needs, the welfare system has an ambiguous role, acting in part to support commodification, and in part to de-commodify needs (Higgs 1993). The problem for health care is that this de-commodification is held fast by the limits set on it by the medicalisation of needs and by the distortion of needs through the discourses of the bargaining process. Quasi-markets played an important part here in that they were a powerful vector for the commodification of needs. The importance of this for future debates on rationing should be apparent.

The concept of ideology is a crucial part of this argument. Ideology, not in the sense of ideas that promote the interests of a particular class or group, but as a critical concept where needs and interests are hidden by the real appearance of distorted forms of thought (Larrain 1994). This interpretation can be contrasted with post-modern critiques of the relationship between ideology and need where it is argued that ideology may explain the fetishism of exchange values but needs and interests are not autonomous realities, but are themselves an effect of exchange value (Baudrillard 1988).[2] If we accept that 'needs talk' is the medium through which political claims are contested in modern society (Fraser 1989), then this post-modern critique gives an elegant account of how reason is crowded out by movements towards discontinuity, fragmentation and the recognition of unlimited particular interests. In this schema, universalist accounts are no longer tenable (Lyotard 1984). Such a position is dependent on the view that it is impossible to judge one discourse from the assumed privileged position of another discourse. This presents us with a contradiction in that by dismissing the validity of a universalist discourse the post-modern critique assumes its own validity (Larrain 1994). Whilst post-modern accounts of change in society are correct in their description of some political and economic trends the danger is that the consequences of change are missed (Taylor-Gooby 1994). In particular the decline of 'reason' runs in parallel with an increase in the social power of the industrial capitalist state (Giddens 1990). This manifests itself in increases in inequality, and in the surveillance and social control of vulnerable groups. Rejecting parts of the post-modernist argument however, does not free us from the problem of how real needs and interests can be distinguished from distorted needs and interests. This book has considered health care needs from the position that a morality is universalist if it recognises as valid only those norms that can be approved in open communicative action (Habermas 1989). The implications of this for health policy is that there has to be a normative domain of procedural guidelines to provide a forum for discussing needs and allocating scarce resources. This is the only way to approach just and fair decision-making:

> For how can one judge the validity of norms, when frequently parties present their own specific interests in a universal guise, under cover of the ideologies of, for example, national interests, civilised behaviour, the new world order, the imperatives of the market, and so on... (Hewitt 1993, p. 68)

It is on the basis of this understanding that the capacity of the system to discuss health care needs and provide appropriate services to meet needs should be evaluated. The question of how such a normative domain can be approximated in practice can not be answered within the confines of this book. However, more innovative ways of commissioning health services that strive for shared understandings are being addressed (Hunter and O'Toole 1995, Doyal 1996). There should be scope for exploring the capacity of advances in information technology to 'democratise' debates around needs. More important perhaps is the need to recognise and counteract the ways in which lay accounts of health are discounted by scientific knowledge (Phillimore and Moffatt 1994).

Conclusion

This book has explored the value of Doyal and Gough's framework for assessing needs and Habermas' communicative ethics for developing a critical analysis of health care decision making. The case of renal services has revealed that where vested interests are able to manipulate discussions, then appeals to need can be used as forms of strategic action. The Habermasian framework built on here has, to some extent, allowed instances of strategic action to be revealed along with the ways in which quasi-markets reinforced the *potential* for strategic action. The problem at the heart of this work, however, is that despite being a valuable framework for evaluating processes it is still questionable whether such communicative procedures *of themselves* can prevent the operation of power with the same success. Indeed the role of the state, in allowing dominant interests the power to control areas like the planning of services and thresholds to care, undermines the ability of an operationalised theory of need to function by means of ethical understandings. The political realities of policy promotes the rhetoric of need whilst implicitly impeding a needs based policy.

Notes

1   In January 1999 the Department of Health consulted on proposals to control the prescribing of Viagra (a treatment for impotence in men). This suggests that rationing is entering a new phase where the government is prepared to make such decisions.

2   For an interesting discussion of these issues in the context of rationing in the NHS see Freemantle and Harrison (1993).

Bibliography

Acheson, R.M. (1978) The definition and identification of need for health care, *Journal of Epidemiology and Community Health,* 32: 1-6.

Acheson, D. (1988) *Public Health in England: The Report of the Committee of inquiry into the future development of public health function,* Chairman Sir Donald Acheson (CM289), London: HMSO.

Acheson, D. (1998) *Independent Inquiry into Inequalities in Health,* London: The Stationery Office.

Alford, R.R. (1975) *Health Care Politics,* Chicago: University of Chicago Press.

Allsop, J. (1984) *Health Policy and the National Health Service,* London: Longman.

Arrow, K.J. (1963) Uncertainty and the welfare economics of medical care, *American Economic Review,* 53.

Arnstein, S. (1969) A ladder of citizen participation, *Journal of the American Institute of Planners,* 35: 216-224.

Avorn, J. (1984) Benefits and Cost analysis in Geriatric Care, *The New England Journal of Medicine,* 310 (20): 1294-1301.

Bachrach, P. and Baratz, M.S. (1970) *Power and Poverty: Theory and Practice,* London: Oxford University Press.

Baker, R. (1993) Visibility and the just allocation of health care: A study of age-rationing in the British National Health Service, *Health Care Analysis,* 1(2): 139-150.

Barr, N. (1987) *The Welfare State as an Efficiency device,* The Welfare State Programme, Suntory Toyota International Centre for Economics and Related Disciplines.

Bartlett, W. and Harrison, L. (1993) Quasi-markets and the National Health Service Reforms, In W.Bartlett and J. Le Grand (eds.) *Quasi-markets and social policy,* London: Macmillan.

Bartley, M. Blane, D. Smith, G.D. (eds.) (1998) *The Sociology of Health Inequalities,* London: Blackwell.

138

Baudrillard, J. (1988) Symbolic exchange and death, in M. Poster (ed.) *Selected Writings*, Cambridge: Polity Press.

Baumol, W. Panzer, J. and Willig, R. (1982) *Contestable markets and the theory of industrial structure*, New York: Harcourt-Brace-Jovanovich.

Beauchamp, T.L. and Childress, J.F. (1989) *Principles of Biomedical Ethics*, Oxford University Press.

Beech, R. Gulliford, M. Mays, N. Melia, J. Roderick, P. Stevens, A. and Raftery, J. (1994) *Health care needs assessment*, Oxford: Radcliffe Press.

Bevan, G (1998) Taking equity seriously: a dilemma for government from allocating resources to primary care groups, *BMJ*, 316: 39-42.

Beveridge, W. (1942) *Report on Social Insurance and Allied Services* (CM 6404), London: HMSO.

Biehal, N. (1993) Changing Practice, *Br J Social Work*, 23: 443-458.

Bolger, P. G. and Davies, R. (1992) Simulation model for planning renal services in a district health authority, *BMJ*, 305: 605-608.

Bourdieu, P. (1991) *Language and symbolic power*, Cambridge: Polity.

Bowling, A. (1993) *What people say about prioritising health services*, London: Kings Fund Centre.

Bradshaw, J.S. (1972) A taxonomy of Social Need in G. Mclachan (ed.) *Problems and Progress in Medical Care*, 7, Nuffield Provincial Hospitals Trust, Oxford University Press.

Bradshaw, J.S. (1994) The conceptualization and measurement of need, A Social Policy perspective, in J. Popay and G. Williams (eds.) *Researching the people's health*, London: Routledge.

Braithwaite, S.S (1993) The courtship of the paying patient, *J Clin Ethics*, 4(2), 124-133.

Branch, R.A. Clark, G.W. Cochrane, A.V. Henry Jones, J. and Scarborough, H. (1971) Incidence of uraemia and requirements for maintenance haemodialysis, *BMJ*, 1: 249-254.

Braybrook, D. (1987) *Meeting Needs*, Princeton NJ: Princeton University Press.

Brearley, S. (1990) *Patient Participation: the literature*, Harrow: Scutari Press.

Buchanan, J.M. (1965) *The inconsistencies of the National Health Service*, Occasional Paper 7, Institute of Economic Affairs.

Buchanan, Allen. E. (1982) *Marx and Justice: The Radical Critique of Liberalism*, Totowa, NJ: Rowman and Littlefield.

Buckingham, K. (1993) A note on HYE (Healthy Years Equivalent), *Journal of Health Economics*, 12 (3): 301-310.

Butler, T and Rowland, M (1998) How will primary care groups work? *BMJ*, 316: 214.

Calnan, M. Halik, J. Sabbat, J. (1998) Citizen participation and patient choice in health reform, in R.E. Saltman, J. Figueras, C. Sakellarides (eds.) *Critical Challenges for Health Care Reform in Europe*, Buckingham: OUP.

Catalano, C. Goodship, T.H.J. Tapson, J.S. Venning, M.K. Taylor, R.M.R. Proud, G. Tunbridge, W.M.G. Elliot, R.W. Ward, M.K. Alberti, K.G.M.M. and Wilkinson, R. (1990) Renal replacement for diabetic patients in Newcastle upon Tyne and the Northern Region, 1964-88, *BMJ*, 301: 535-540.

Chalmers, I. (1995) Letter, What would Archie Cochrane have said?, *Lancet*, 346:1300.

Charles, C. DeMaio, S. (1993) Lay participation in health care decision making, *Journal of Health Politics Policy and Law*, 18 (4): 881-904.

Charney M.C. Lewis P.A. Farrow S.C, (1989), Choosing who shall not be treated in the NHS, *Soc Sci Med*, 28 (12): 1331-1338.

Coast, J. (1997) The rationing debate: rationing within the NHS should be explicit: The case against, *BMJ*, 314: 1118.

Cochrane, A. (1971) *Effectiveness and Efficiency*. London: Nuffield Provincial Hospitals Trust.

Cohen, J. (1986) Review of Spheres of Justice, *Journal of Philosophy*, 83(8), 457-468.

Coulter, A. Mays, N. (1997) Deregulating primary care. *BMJ*, 314: 510-513.

Craft, N. (1994) The rise of Stalinism in the NHS, *BMJ*, 309: 1640-1645.

Culyer, A.J. (1976) *Need and the NHS*, London: Martin Robertson.

Culyer, A.J. (1980) *The Political Economy of Social Policy*, Oxford: Martin Robertson.

Culyer A.J. (1991) *Health, health expenditures and equity*, Discussion paper 83, Centre for Health Economics, University of York.

Culyer, A.J. Donaldson, C. and Gerard, K. (1988) *Working Party on alternative delivery and funding of Health Services*, IHSM working paper number 2.

Culyer, A.J. Maynard, A.K. and Posnett, J.W. (eds.) (1990) *Competition in Health Care, Reforming the NHS*, Basingstoke: Macmillan.

Culyer, A.J. and Wagstaff, A. (1991) *Need, Equality and Social Justice*, Discussion paper 90, Centre for Health Economics, University of York.

Culyer, A.J. and Wagstaff, A. (1992) *Need, Equity and Equality in Health Care*, Discussion paper 95, Centre for Health Economics, University of York.

Culyer, A. J. and Wagstaff, A. QALYs versus HYEs, (1993) *Journal of Health Economics*, 12 (3): 311-324.

Curtis, S. (1989) *The Geography of Public Welfare Provision*, London, New York: Routledge.

Dalziell, M. and Garret, C. (1987) Intraregional variation in treatment of end stage renal failure. *BMJ*, 294: 1382-1383.

Daniels, N. (1985) *Just Health Care*, Cambridge: Cambridge University Press.

Daniels, N. (1991) Is the Oregon Rationing Plan Fair? JAMA, 265 (17): 2232-2235.

De Jong, G. and Rutten, F.F.H. (1983) Justice and health for all, *Social Science and Medicine*, 17: 1085-1095.

Department of Health, (1989a) *Working for Patients* (CM555), London: HMSO.

Department of Health, (1989b) Contracts for Health Services: Operational Principles, EL(89), MB/169.

Department of Health, (1990) *Starting Specifications*, a DHA project paper.

Department of Health, (1991) *Moving Forward; Needs Services and Contracts*, a DHA project paper.

Department of Health, (1996) *Patient Partnership Strategy*, NHS Executive.

Department of Health, (1997) *The New NHS, modern, dependable*, London: The Stationery Office.

Donaldson, C. and Mooney, G. (1991) *Needs assessment, priority setting, and contracts for health care: an economic view*; HERU Discussion paper 05/91, University of Aberdeen.

Doyal, L. (1979) *The political economy of health*. London: Pluto.

Doyal, L. and Gough, I. (1984) A theory of Human Needs, *Critical Social Policy* 4(1): 6-38.

Doyal, L. and Gough, I. (1991) *A Theory of Human Need*, Basingstoke: Macmillan Education Ltd.

Doyal, L. (1992) Need for moral audit in evaluating quality in health care, *Quality in Health Care*,1:178-183.

Doyal, L. (1993) Thinking about human need, *New Left Review*, 201: 113-128.

Doyal, L. (1996) Needs, rights, and equity: moral quality in healthcare rationing, *Quality in health care*, 4: 273-83.

Doyal, L. (1997) The rationing debate: rationing within the NHS should be explicit: The case for, *BMJ*, 314: 1114.

Drummond, M.F. (1980) *Principles of economic appraisal in Health Care*, Oxford: Oxford Medical Publications.

Dworkin, R. (1977) *Taking Rights seriously*, Duckworth (1991 sixth impression).

Dworkin, R. (1981) What is Equality? *Philosophy and Public Affairs*, 10: 4.

Dworkin, R. (1983) In defense of Equality, *Social Philosophy and Policy*, 1 (1).

Eddy, D.M. (1984) Variations in physician practice: the role of uncertainty. *Health Affairs*, 3 (2): 74-89.

Edgeworth, B. (1992) Reading Dworkin Empirically: Principles, Policies and Property, in A. Hunt (ed.), *Reading Dworkin Critically*, Oxford: Berg Publishers.

Enthoven, A. (1985) *Reflections on the Management of the National Health Service*, Occasional Papers (5), London: Nuffield Provincial Hospitals Trust.

Enthoven, A. (1991) Internal Market Reform of the British National Health Service, *Health Affairs*, Fall, 61 - 70.

European Dialysis and Transplant Registry, (1988) Demography of dialysis and transplantation in Europe in 1985 and 1986: Trends over the previous decade, *Nephrol,Dial,Transplant,* 3: 714-727.

Evans, R. G. (1990) The dog in the night time: Medical practice variations and health policy, in T.F. Anderson and G. Mooney (eds.) *The challanges of medical practice variations,* Basingstoke: Macmillan Press Ltd.

Feest, T. G. and Harrison, P. (1992) Simulation model for planning renal services, Letter, *BMJ,* 305: 1018.

Feest, T.G. Mistry, C. Grimes, D.S. and Mallick, N.P. (1990) Incidence of advanced chronic renal failure and the need for end stage renal replacement treatment, *BMJ,* 301: 897-900.

Fitzpatrick, R. (1987) Political Science and Health Policy, in G. Scambler, (ed.), *Sociological Theory and Medical Sociology;* London and New York: Tavistock Publications.

Forde-Roberts, V.J. (1998) *Working for Patients? An analysis of some effects of the National Health Service reforms in South Buckinghamshire.* Unpublished PhD thesis, QMW, University of London.

Foucault, M. (1980) *Power/Knowledge: Selected Interviews and other writings 1972-1977,* C. Gordon, (ed.) Brighton: The Harvester Press.

Foucault, M. (1982) The subject and Power, afterword in H. Dreyfus and P. Rabinow, *Michael Foucault - Beyond Structuralism and Hermeneutics,* Brighton: The Harvester Press.

Fox, D.M. Leichter, H.M. (1991) Rationing care in Oregon: The New Accountability, *Health Affairs,* 10 (2): 7-27.

Frankel, S. (1991) Health needs, health care requirements and the myth of infinite demand, *The Lancet,* 337: 1588-1589.

Frankel, S. West, R. (1993) *Rationing and Rationality in the National Health Service; The persistence of waiting lists,* London: Macmillan Press Ltd.

Fraser, N. (1981) Foucault on Modern Power: Empirical insights and Normative Confusions, *Praxis International,* 1: 283.

Fraser, N. (1989) *Unruly practices, Power discourse and gender in contemporary social theory,* Cambridge: Polity Press.

Freemantle, N. and Harrison, S. (1993) Interlukin-2: the public and professional face of rationing in the NHS, *Critical Social Policy,* 37: 94-117.

Friedman, M. and Friedman, R. (1980) *Free to Choose,* Hamondsworth: Penguin.

Friedson, E. (1986) *Professional Powers. A study of the institutionalisation of formal knowledge,* Chicago Ill: University of Chicago Press.

Friss, L. Friedman, B. and Demakis, J. (1989) Geographic differences in the use of Veterans Administration Hospitals, *Soc Sci Med,* 28 (4): 347-354.

Geras, N. (1983) *Marx and Human Nature: refutation of a Legend,* London: Verso.

Giddens, A (1971) *Capitalism and modern social theory: an analysis of the writings of Marx, Durkheim and Max Weber,* Cambridge University Press.

Giddens, A. (1982) *Profiles and Critiques in Social Theory,* London: Macmillan.

Giddens, A. (1990) *The Social Consequences of Modernity,* Cambridge: Polity Press.

Gilligan, C. (1987) Moral Orientation and Moral Development, in E. Kittay and D. Mayers (eds.) *Women and Moral theory,* Savage: Rowman and Littlefield.

Glaser, W. (1993) The competition vogue and its outcomes, *Lancet,* 341: 805-12.

Goodin, R.E. (1988) *Reasons for Welfare, The Political Theory of the Welfare State,* Princeton University Press.

Gore, S.M. Hinds, C.J. and Rutherford, A.J. (1989) Organ donation from intensive care units in England, *BMJ,* 299: 1193-1197.

Gough, I. (1979) *The Political Economy of the Welfare State,* Basingstoke: Macmillan Eduction Ltd.

Gough, I. and Thomas, T. (1994) Needs Satisfaction and Welfare Outcomes: Theory and Explanations, *Social Policy and Administration,* 28 (1): 33-56.

Gray, J. (1988) Against Cohen on proletarian unfreedom, *Social Philosophy and Policy,* 6 (1): 77-86, 94-112.

Gray, J. (1992) *The Moral Foundations of Market Institutions,* IEA Health and Welfare Unit, Choice in wefare No 10, IEA.

Green, D. (1986) *Challenge to the NHS: A study of competition in American Health Care and the Lessons for Britain,* London: Institute of Economic Affairs.

Greenwood, R.N. (1993) Quality in Dialysis, Presentation to the *Renal Conference,* April 1993.

Greenwood, R.N. Aldridge, C. Farrington, K. and Tattesall, J.E. (1992) Quality standards in dialysis: advice to purchasers, *THS,* May 1992.

Griffiths, R. (1983) *NHS Management Enquiry Report,* London: DHSS.

Guadagnoli, E. and Ward, P. (1998) Patient participation in Decision-Making, *Social Science and Medicine,* 47 (3): 329-339.

Habermas, J. (1979) *Communication and the Evolution of Society,* London: Heinemann.

Habermas, J. (1984) *The Theory of Communicative Action Vol 1, Reason and the Rationalisation of Society.* London: Heineman.

Habermas, J. (1989) *The New Conservatism: Cultural Criticism and the Historians' Debate,* Cambridge: Polity Press.

Habermas, J. (1990) *Moral Consciousness and Communicative Action,* Cambridge: Polity Press.

Habermas, J. (1992) *The philosophical Discourse of Modernity,* Cambridge: Polity Press.

Hadorn, D.C. (1991) Setting Health Care priorities in Oregon, cost-effectiveness meets the rule of rescue. Special communication *JAMA,* 265,17.

Halper, T. (1989) *The misfortune of others: End Stage Renal Disease in the United Kingdom,* Cambridge: Cambridge University Press.

Ham, C. (1985) *Health policy in Britain,* 2nd Edition, London: Macmillan.

Ham, C. and Hill, M. (1984) *The Policy Process in the Modern Capitalist State,* New York: Harvester Wheatsheaf.

Ham, C. (1995) Synthesis: what can we learn from international experience? *British Medical Bulletin,* 51 (4): 819-830.

Ham, C. and Honigsbaum, F. (1998) Priority setting and rationing health services, in R.B. Saltman, J.Figueras and C. Sakellarides (eds.) *Critical challenges for Health Care reform in Europe,* Buckinham: OUP.

Hardy, M. A. Kiernan, J. Kutscher, A.H. Cahill, L. and Benvenisty, A.I. (eds.) (1991) *Psychosocial Aspects of End-Stage Renal Disease, Issues of our Times,* New York: The Haworth Press.

Harris, J. (1985) *The value of life,* London: Routledge and Kegan Paul.

Harris, R. (1988) *Beyond the Welfare State, An economic, political and moral critique of indiscriminate state welfare, and a review of alternatives to dependency,* Occasional Paper 77, Institute of Economic Affairs.

Harrison, S. Hunter, D.J. and Pollitt, C. J. (1990) *The Dynamics of British Health Policy,* London: Unwin Hyman.

Harrison, S. (1991) Purchasers, providers and competition in the NHS, *British Hospital Management Annual Review of British Hospital and Health Care Planning and Development 1992,* Sterling Publications, 40-42.

Harrison, S. Hunter, D. Marnoch, D. and Pollit, C. (1992) *Just Managing: Power and Culture in the National Health Service, Basingstoke:* Macmillan Press Ltd.

Hart, J.T. (1971) The Inverse care Law, *Lancet,* 2: 405-412.

Hart, L.G. and Evans, R.W. (1987) The functional status of ESRD patients as measured by the Sickness Impact Profile, *J Chron Dis,* 40 (Suppl 1): 117S-130S.

Harvey, D. (1989) *The Condition of Postmodernity, An Enquiry into the Origins of Cultural Change,* Oxford: Basil Blackwell.

Hayek, F.A. (1944) *The Road to Serfdom,* London: Routledge and Kegan Paul.

Heath, I. (1997) The threat to social justice, *BMJ,* 314: 598-599.

Heginbotham, C. Ham, C. Cochrane, M. and Richards, J. (1992) *Purchasing Dilemmas,* London: Kings Fund college and Southampton and South West Hampshire Health Authority.

Hewitt, M. (1993) Social movements and social need: problems with postmodern political theory, *Critical Social Policy,* 37: 52-74.

Higgs, P. (1993) *The NHS and Ideological Conflict,* Aldershot: Avebury.

Hindess, B. (1987) *Freedom, Equality and the Market. Arguments on Social Policy*, London: Tavistock Publications.

Horton, R (1998) The realpolitik of a new National Health Service for the UK, *Lancet*, 351: 76-77.

Hunt, A. (1992) Law's Empire or Legal Imperialism, in A. Hunt (ed.) *Reading Dworkin Critically*, Oxford: Berg Publishers.

Hunter D.J. (1995) Rationing health care: the political perspective, *British Medical Bulletin*, 51 (**4**): 876-884.

Hunter, D. and O'Toole, S. (1995) rosy outlook, *Health Service Journal*, 11th May 1995: 20-22.

Hutchinson, A.C. (1992) The Last Emperor, in A. Hunt, (ed.) *Op cit.*

Iliffe, S. Munro, J. (1993) General Practitioners and incentives, *BMJ*, 307: 1156-1157.

Illich, I. (1976) *Limits To Medicine Medical Nemesis: The Expropriation of Health*, Harmondsworth Middlesex: Pelican Books.

Jacobson, B. (1996) *Health in the East End*, press release to annual public health report 1996/97, East London and the City Health Authority.

Jones, I.R. (1992) Oregon, Public Health and Social Control, *Critical Public Health*, 3 (2): 12-16.

Jones, I.R. (1995a) Health Care Need and Contracts for Health Services, *Health Care Analysis*, 3 (2): 91-98.

Jones, I.R. (1995b) *Health Care Needs and Health Policy: The Case of Renal Services*, Unpublished PhD Thesis, London: University of London.

Kearns, D. (1983) A Theory of Justice and Love; Rawls on the Family, *Politics* 18 (2): 36-42.

Keat, R. (1981) *The politics of Social Theory*, Oxford: Blackwell.

Kelson, M. (1995) *Consumer involvement in clinical audit and outcomes*, London: College of Health.

Kennedy, I. (1983) *The Unmasking of medicine*, London: Paladin.

Kilner, J.F. (1990) *Who Lives? Who Dies? Ethical criteria in patient selection*, New Haven and London: Yale University Press.

Klein, R. (1983) *The Politics of the National Health Service*, London: Longman Group Limited.

Klein, R. (1991) On the Oregon Trail: rationing health care (editorial), *BMJ*, 302 (6767): 1-2.

Klein, R. Day, P. Redmayne, S. (1996) Managing Scarcity, *Priority Setting and Rationing in the National Health Service*, Buckingham: OUP.

Kornblum, W. (1974) *Blue collar community*, Chicago: University of Chicago Press.

Kutner, N.G. Brogan, D. and Kutner, M.H. (1986) End Stage renal disease treatment modality and patients quality of life, *American Journal Nephrology*, 6: 396-402.

Kymliska, W. (1990) The Public and the Private, in *Contemporary Political Philosophy: An Introduction*, pp. 247-62, Oxford: Oxford University Press.

Labour party (1994) *Health 2000*, London: Labour Party.

Lancet (1995) Evidence-based medicine, in its place, *Lancet*, 346: 785.

Lancet, (1993) A "life" no longer supported, *Lancet*, 341: 410.

Lancet, (1990) Organ donors in the UK getting the numbers right, *Lancet*, 335: 80-82.

Larrain, J. (1994) The postmodern critique of ideology, *The Sociological Review*, 42 (2): 289-314.

Last, J.M. (1963) The Iceberg: Completing the clinical picture in General practice, *Lancet*, 2: 28-31.

Le Grand, J. (1987) *Three Essays on equity*, Welfare State programme, Discussion paper 23, Suntory Toyota International Centre for Economics and related disciplines.

Le Grand, J. (1990) Equity versus Efficiency: The Elusive Trade-off, *Ethics*, 100: 554-568.

Levy, B.H. (1977) Power and Sex: An Interview with Michael Foucault, *Telos*, 32: 152-161.

Light, D.W. (1992) Equity and Efficiency in Health Care, *Soc Sci Med*, 35 (4): 465-469.

Light, D.W. (1993) Escaping the traps of post-war Western medicine, How to maximise health and minimize happiness, *European Journal of Public Health*, 3: 281-289.

Light, D.W. May, A.M.E. (eds.) (1993) *From Welfare State to Managed Market: The transformation of British Health Care*, Washington: Faulkner and Gray.

Lindblom, C.E. (1959) The Science of Muddling Through, *Public Administration Review*, 19 (3): 79-88.

Lindblom, C.E. (1979) Still Muddling, Not Yet Through, *Public Administration Review*, 39 (6): 517-26.

Lipsky, M. (1980) *Street Level Bureaucracy*, New York: Russel Sage Foundation.

Liss, P.E. (1993) *Health Care Need, Meaning and Measurement*, Aldershot: Avebury.

Lowy, M. (1979) *Georg Lukacs - From Romantic to Revolutionary*, London: New Left Books.

Ludbrook, A. (1985) The economics of home care for the treatment of end stage renal failure. *Int J Tech Asses Health care*, 1: 315-324.

Lukes, S. (1974) *Power: A Radical View*, London: Macmillan.

Lukes, S. (1982) Of gods and demons: Habermas and practical reason in J. Thompson and D. Held (eds.), *Habermas*, London: Macmillan.

Lyotard, J-F. (1984) *The Postmodern Condition: A Report on Knowledge*, Manchester: Manchester University Press.

Mancini, P.V. (1983) The economics of diabetic nephropathy, *Diabetic Nephropathy*, 2: 4-7.

Marmot, M.G. (1989) Social Class and Mortality *Trends and explanations, in Socio Economic Inequalities in Health, questions on trends and explanations*, L.J. Gunning-Schepters, I.P. Spruit and J.H. Krijnene (eds.) The Hauge: Ministry of Welfare, Health and Cultural Affairs.

Maxwell, R. (ed.) (1995) *Rationing health care*, London: Churchill Livingstone.

Mays, N.B. (1990) *Management and resource allocation in end stage renal failure units: a review of current issues*, King Edward's hospital fund for London.

McCormick, M.G. and Navarro, V. (1973) Prevalence of Chronic renal failure and access to dialysis, *International Journal of Epidemiology*, 2: 247.

McEwen, J. et al (1983) *Participation in health*, London: Croon Helm.

McGeown, M.G. (1990) Prevalence of advanced renal failure in Northern Ireland, *BMJ*, 301: 900-903.

Mckeown, T. (1979) *The Role of Medicine - Dream Mirage or Nemesis* Oxford: Basil Blackwell.

Meherez, A. and Gafni, A (1989) Quality-adjusted life years, utility theory, and healthy-years equivalents, *Medical Decision Making*, 9: 142-149.

Melia, J. Beech, R. and Swan, T. (1991) Incidence of advanced Renal Failure, *BMJ*, 302: 51-52.

Mercer, A. (1990) *Disease Mortality and population in transition, epidemiological-demographic change in England since the eighteenth century as part of a global phenomenon*, Leicester: Leicester University Press.

Mitroff, I.I. (1983) *Stakeholders of the organizational mind*, San Francisco: Josey Bass Publishers.

Montgomery, J. (1992) Rights to Health and Health care, chapter in, *The welfare of Citizens*, A. Coote (ed.), IPPR/Rivers Oram Press.

Mooney, G.H. (1986) *Economics, medicine and health care*, London: Harvester Wheatsheaf.

Mooney, G.H. and McGuire, A. (1987) What does equity in health mean? *World Health Statistical Quarterly*, No 4.

Mooney, G.H. and Loft, A. (1989) Clinical decision making and health care policy: what is the link?, *Health Policy*, II: 19-25.

Munzer, S.R. (1990) *A Theory of Property*, New York: Cambrdige University Press.

Navarro, V. (1978) *Class Struggle, The State and Medicine*, London: Mark Robertson.

New, B. (1996) The rationing agenda in the NHS, *BMJ*, 312: 1593-1601.

New, B. and Le Grand, J. (1996) *Rationing in the NHS, Principles and Pragmatism*, London: King's Fund.

Netherlands. (1992) *A report by the Government Committee on choices in Health Care*, The Netherlands: Ministry of welfare and cultural affairs.

Niskanen, W.A. (1971) *Bureaucracy and Representative Government*, Chicago: Aldine-Atherton.

North East Thames Regional Health Authority, (1990) *A discussion document for Renal Replacement Services*, March 1990.

Nozick, R. (1974) *Anarchy , State and Utopia*, Oxford: Basil Blackwell.

O'Connor, J. (1973) *The Fiscal Crisis of the State*, New York: St Martin's Press.

Offe, C. (1984) *Contradicitons of the Welfare State*, London: Hutchinson.

Offe, C. (1985) *Disorganised Capitalism*, Cambridge: Polity Press.

Okin, S. M. (1989) Reason and Feeling in Thinking about Justice, *Ethics*, 99 (2): 229-249.

Oliver, M. (1990) *The Politics of Disablement*, Basingstoke: Macmillan.

OPCS, (1988) *The prevalence of disability among adults*, Report 1, HMSO.

Parsons, V. and Lock, P.M. (1980), Triage and the patient with renal failure, *Journal of medical ethics*, 6: 173-176.

Peffer, R.G. (1990) *Marxism, Moralty and Social Justice*, Princeton University Press.

Penz, G. (1986) *Consumer Sovereignty and human interests*, Cambridge: Cambridge University Press.

Percy-Smith, J. Sanderson, I. (1992) *Understanding Local Needs*, IPPR.

Pereira, J. (1990a) *What does Equity in Health Care Mean?* Discussion Paper 61, Centre for Health Economics, University of York.

Pereira, J. (1990b) The economics of inequality in health: A Bibilography, *Soc Sci Med*, 31 (3): 413-420.

Philip, M. (1985) Michael Foucault, in Q Skinner (ed.) *The Return of Grand Theory in the Human Sciences*, Canto (1990 edition).

Phillimore, P. Beattie, A. and Townsend, P. (1994) Widening inequality in northern England, 1981-91, *BMJ*, 308: 1125-1128.

Phillimore, P. and Moffatt, S. (1994) Discounted knowledge, Local experience, environmental pollution and health, in J, Popay and G, Williams (eds.) *Researching the people's health*, London: Routledge.

Pile, S. (1990) Depth Hermeneutics and critical human geography, *Environment and Planning D: Society and Space*, 8: 211-232.

Plant, R. (1992) Citizenship, Rights and Welfare, in A. Coote (ed.) *The Welfare of Citizens, Developing new social rights*, IPPR, London: Rivers Oram Press.

Pogge, T.W. (1989) *Realising Rawls*, Ithaca: Cornell University Press.

Poulantzas, N. (1978) *State, Power and Socialism* , London: New Left Books.

Poulter, D. (1993) *Great Expectations*, paper presented to The Renal Conference, Choices for the future in renal services 21st April 1993.

Powell, J.E. (1966) *Medicine and Politics*, London: Pitman Medical.

PSI. (1993) *Rationing Health and Health care*, London: PSI.

Purviance, S.M. (1993) Kidney transplantation policy: race and distributive justice, Business and professional ethics journal, 12(2).

Rabinow, P. (1984) *The Foucault Reader: An Introduction to Foucault's thought*, London: Penguin Books.

Rawls, J. (1972) *A Theory of Justice*, Oxford: Oxford University Press.

Rawls, J. (1980) Kantian Constructivism in Moral Theory, *Journal of Philosophy*, 77: 525-527, 554.

Raz, J. (1986) *The Morality of freedom*, Oxford: Oxford University Press.

Relman, A.S. (1990) The trouble with rationing, *N Eng J Med*, 323: 911-913.

Renal Association, (1991) *The provision of services for adult patients with renal disease in the United Kingdom*, London: Renal Association.

Renal Review Group, (1993) *Report of the Review of the London Renal Services*, HMSO.

Rennie, D. Retting, R.A. and Wing, A.J. (1985) Limited resources and the treatment of end stage renal failure in Britain and the United States, *Q.J. Med*, 56: 321-336.

Resource Allocation Working Party, (1976) *Sharing resources for health in England, Report of the Resource Allocation Working Party*, London: DHSS.

Roberts, J. (1992) The drama of the NHS, *Critical Public Health*, 3 (1): 35-41.

Roberts, J. (1993) Managing Markets, *Journal of Public Health Medicine*, 15, 4: 305-310.

Roos, L.L. Brazouskas, R. Cohen, M.M. Sharp, S.M. (1990) Variations in Outcome Research, in T.F. Anderson and G. Mooney (eds.) *The challenges of Medical Practice Variations*, Basingstoke: Macmillan Press.

Salter, B. (1993) The Politics of purchasing in the National Health Service, *Policy and Politics*, 21 (3): 171-184.

Salter, B. (1998) *The politics of change in the health service*, Basingstoke: Macmillan.

Sandel, M. (1982) *Liberalism and the Limits of Justice*, Cambridge: Cambridge University Press, 28-35.

Sandel, M. (1984) *Liberalism and its critics*, London: Basil Blackwell.

Scambler, G. (1987) Habermas and the power of medical expertise, in G. Scambler (ed.) *Sociological Theory and Medical Sociology*, London: Tavistock.

Schlosberg, D. (1995) Communicative Action in Practice: Intersubjectivity and New Social Movements, *Political Studies*, XLIII, 291-311.

Schmitter, P.C. (1974) Still the century of Corporatism? *Review of Politics*, 36: 85-131.

Schwartz, D. (1959) *Summer knowledge*, New York: New Directions books.

Secretary of State, (1989) Speech on role of DHAs for conference on Shaping the Nations Health, December, *EL (89)* MB/219.

Seedhouse, D. (1994) *Fortress NHS, A Philosophical Review of the National Health Service*, Chichester: John Wiley and Sons Ltd.

149

Sen, A. (1985) *Commodities and Capabilites*, Amsterdam: North Holland.

Sen, A. (1987) Justice in J. Eatwell, M. Milgate, P. Newman (eds.) *The New Palgrave: A dictionary of Economics*, Basingstoke: MacMillan.

Sen, A. (1992) *Inequality Re-examined*, Cambridge Mass: Harvard University Press.

Seymour, W. (1989) *Bodily alterations, an introduction to a sociology of the body for health workers*, London: Allen & Unwin.

Sheaff, R. (1996) *The need for healthcare*, London: Routledge.

Silverman, D. (1985) *Qualitative methodology and sociology, describing the social world*, Aldershot: Gower.

Simmons, R.G. Mrine, K.S. (1984) The regulation of high cost technology medicine: the case of dialysis and transplantation in the United Kingdom, *Journal of Health and Social Behaviour*; 25 (September): 320-334.

Simmons, R.G. Abress, L. and Anderson, C.R. (1988) Quality of life after kidney transplantation: a prospective randomised comparison of cyclosporine and conventional immunosuppressive therapy, *Transplantation*, 45: 415-421.

Smith, I. (1994) West Yorkshire Initiative, *Commissioning Health Care for People with End Stage Renal Failure: a layman's guide*, Leeds: Nuffield Institute for Health.

Smith R (1996) Rationing health care: moving the debate forward, *BMJ*, 312: 1553-1554.

Smith, W.G.C. Cohen, D.R. and Asscher, A.W. (1989) *Evaluation of renal services in Wales with particular reference to the role of subsidiary units.* Dept of renal medicine, KRUF Institute of Renal Disease, Royal Infirmary, Cardiff: Report to the Welsh Office.

Soper, K. (1981) *On Human Needs*, Brighton: Harvester.

Soper, K. (1993) A theory of Human Need, *New Left Review*, 197: 113-128.

Steele, R. (1981) Marginal met need and geographical equity in health care, *Scottish Journal of Political Economy*, 28.

Steele, R. (1989) *Management issues in renal failure.* A study carried out for the DHSS.

Stevens, A. (1991) Needs Assessment needs assessment, *Health Trends*, 23: 20-23.

Szreter, S. (1988) The importance of social intervention in Britain's mortality decline c 1850-1914: a reinterpretation of the role of public health, *Soc History Med*, 1: 1-38.

Taylor-Gooby, P. (1985) The politics of welfare: public attitudes and behaviour, in R.E. Klein and M. O'Higgins (eds.) *The future of Welfare*, pp. 72-91, Oxford: Blackwell.

Taylor-Gooby, P. (1994) Postmodernism and Social Policy: A Great Leap Backwards? *Jnl Soc Pol*, 23 (3): 385-404.

ten Have, H.A.M.J. and Loughlin, M. (1994) Responsibilities and Rationalities: Should the Patient be blamed?, *Health Care Analysis*, 2: 119-127.

Thatcher, M. (1989) Foreword to *Working for Patients*, CM555, London: HMSO.

Thompson, J. (1981) *Critical Hermeneutics: A study in the thought of Paul Ricoeur and Jurgen Habermas*, Cambridge: Cambridge University Press .

Thompson, J. (1984) Rationality and social rationalization:an assessment of Habermas' theory of communicative action, in J Thompson, *Studies in the Theory of Ideology*, Oxford: Polity Press.

Thomson, G. (1987) *Needs*, London: Routledge and Kegan Paul.

Thwaites, Sir Bryan. (1987) *The NHS:The end of the rainbow?*, *The Foundation lecture*, The University of Southampton, Institute of Health Policy Studies.

The Times, (1994) Patients dying for want of dialysis as machines lie idle, p. 5, *24th January* 1994.

Titmuss, R.M. (1968) *Commitment to welfare*, London: Allen and Unwin.

Tomlinson, Sir Bernard. (1992) *Report of the Inquiry into London's Health Service, medical education and Research*, HMSO, October 1992.

Townsend, P. Davidson, N. (1982) *Inequalities in Health, The Black Report*, London: Penguin Books Ltd.

Townsend, P. (1993) *The International Analysis of Poverty*, London: Harvester Wheatsheaf.

Turnberg, L. (1997) *Strategic Review into London's health services*, London, Stationery Office.

Turner, B (1993) *Max Weber: From History to Modernity*, London: Routledge.

Turner, B (1996) *For Weber: Essays on the Sociology of Fate*, London: Sage.

Wagstaff, A. (1991) QALYs and the equity-efficiency trade-off, *Journal of Health Economics*, 10: 21-41.

Waldron, J. (1984) *Theories of Rights, Oxford Readings in Philosophy*, Oxford: Oxford University Press.

Walzer, M. (1983) *Spheres of Justice*, Oxford:Blackwell.

Walzer, M. (1990) The Communitarian Critique of Liberalism, *Ethics*, 99 (4): 52-82.

Waterworth, S. and Luker, K.A. (1990) Reluctant collaborators. Do patients want to be involved in decision concerning care? *Journal of Advanced Nursing*, 15: 971-976.

Weber, M (1978) *Economy and Society* (2 vols) Berkeley: University of California Press.

Webster, C. (1995) The making of the National Health Service, *Modern History Review*, 6 (4): 11-13.

Webster, C. (1998) *The National Health Service: A PoliticalHistory*, Oxford: OUP.

West, R. (1991) *Organ Transplantation*, London: Office of Health Economics.

White, S.K. (1988) *The recent work of Jurgen Habermas, Reason, Justice and modernity*, Cambridge: Cambridge University Press.

Whitehead, M. (1987) *The Health Divide: Inequalities in health in the 1980's*, Health Education Council.

Wiggins, D. and Dermen, S. (1987) Needs, need, needing, *Journal of medical ethics*, 13: 62-68.

Williams, A. (1978) 'Need' an Economic Exegis, in A. Culyer,and K.Wright (eds.) *Economic Aspects of Health Services*, London: Martin Robertson.

Williams, A. (1985) Economics of coronary artery bypass grafting, *BMJ*, 291: 326-329.

Williams, G. and Popay, J. (1994) Researching the People's Health, Dilemmas and opportunites for social scientists in J. Popay and G. Williams (eds.) *Researching the People's Health*, London: Routledge.

Williamson, O. (1975) *Markets and Hierarchies: Analysis and Antitrust Implications*, New York: The Free Press.

Wing, A.J. (1983) Why don't the British treat more patients with Kidney Failure?, *BMJ*, 287: 1157-1158.

Wing, A.J. (1990), Can we meet the real need for dialysis and transplantation?, *BMJ*, 301: 885-886.

Wing, A.J. (1993) Ageism in British Renal Units: A view from inside the system, *Health Care Analysis*, 1 (2): 151-152.

Wing, A.J. Broyer, M. and Brunner, F.P. (1982) EDTA registry analyses, in B. Bradley and D. Moras (eds.) *UK Transplant Service Review 1982*, Bristol: UK Transplant service.

Wood, A. (1981) Marx and Equality, in J. Mepham and D. Ruben (eds.) *Issues in Marxist Philosophy*, 4, Brighton: Harvester Press.

Wood, I.T. Mallick, N.P. and Moores, B. (1980) A flexible model for planning facilities for patients with end-stage renal failure *BMJ*, 281: 575-577.

Wood, I.T. Mallick, N.P. and Wing, A.J. (1987) Prediction of resources needed to achieve the national target for treatment of renal failure, *BMJ* (Clin Res) 294: 1467-1470.

Yates, J. (1995) *Private Eye, Heart and Hip*, Edinburgh: Churchill Livingstone.

Young, M. (1989) A place for vouchers in the NHS, *Samizdat*, 6: 4-5.

Zola, I.K. (1972) *Medicine as an institution of social control: the medicalizing of society*, in D. Tuckett and J. Kaufert, (1978) *Basic Readings in Medical Sociology*, London: Tavistock Publications Limited.